James T. (James Thomas) Edwards, John McDonogh

Some interesting Papers of John McDonogh

Chiefly concerning the Louisiana Purchase and the Liberian Colonization

James T. (James Thomas) Edwards, John McDonogh

Some interesting Papers of John McDonogh
Chiefly concerning the Louisiana Purchase and the Liberian Colonization

ISBN/EAN: 9783337152734

Printed in Europe, USA, Canada, Australia, Japan

Cover: Foto ©ninafisch / pixelio.de

More available books at **www.hansebooks.com**

Some Interesting Papers

of

John McDonogh

Chiefly concerning the Louisiana Purchase
and
The Liberian Colonization

Edited by James T. Edwards, D. D., LL. D.

Printed by Boys of McDonogh School
McDonogh, Maryland
1898.

INTRODUCTION.

Although extracts have been made from two or three of the letters which follow, it is believed that none of them, with one exception, has heretofore been published in full.

They afford aid in forming a just estimate of the mental abilities and moral traits of John McDonogh.

He was no ordinary man, but cast in an original mold, singularly self-centered, and masterful, but withal something of a dreamer. Even to this day somewhat of mystery surrounds his character, and for a long time during his life he was misunderstood and misjudged. Born in Baltimore December 29, 1779 of that Scotch-Irish stock which has furnished a forceful element of our population wherever found, he always displayed the combination of practical good sense and imagination which are characteristic of that race. He died in McDonoghville, La., October 26, 1850.

His parents were highly respectable people in good circumstances. Shortly after reaching his majority he went to New Orleans, and from that time forward was almost entirely deprived of the companionship of his immediate relatives, and he never knew the love of wife and children. Under a calm, somewhat stern exterior burned a quenchless enthusiasm for the attainment of certain noble ends to which he devoted all the energies of his being. To secure these he deemed it necessary that his plans should be matured in secret, and this was the chief reason why his conduct was misunderstood.

Two of these great objects were, first, a far-reaching plan of education, and second, the liberation of his slaves; the former of these was not known until after his death, and the latter was locked in his own heart and the hearts of his bondmen for many years. Solitary and alone he wrought out his projects for the completion of his lofty purposes. It must not be supposed, however, that in the meantime he did not prominently participate in the activities that pertained to his station as a man of wealth. He was constantly interested in the education of youth, and displayed a fair degree of liberality towards the benevolences of his time, but his posthumous fame for good works far surpasses his reputation for philanthropy during his lifetime.

The success of his educational scheme is now well known and need not here be dwelt upon, except to say that he left a fortune which finally yielded nearly a million dollars to each of the cities New Orleans and Baltimore. These sums have been devoted to the improvement of youth, particularly of the deserving poor.

The letters in this pamphlet relate especially, however, to two other objects which greatly enlisted his interest; namely, the settlement of the great questions growing out of the Louisiana Purchase, and the colonization of the colored man in Liberia.

McDonogh was an ardent patriot; he fought for his country in 1812, and had a firm faith in its future greatness. For quite a portion of his life he was perhaps the ablest champion who contended for the rights of settlers who had become owners of land included in the Louisiana and the Florida Purchase. His discussion in regard to the validity of titles thus obtained was characterized by distinguished ability, and the battle which he waged in behalf of the people has never yet been adequately recognized. He never faltered in this fight, although he did not live to see the complete victory. The validity of these land titles in dispute in Louisiana and West Florida was finally decided by the Supreme Court of the United States, January 9, 1874.

The ability which he displayed in maintaining the validity of the Spanish land-titles issued before the actual occupation of Eastern Louisiana and West Florida by the United States "commended him to a large portion of his fellow citizens as a proper person to represent their interests in the United States Senate, but he was defeated by a small majority."

The "Mr. Livingston" referred to in Mr. McDonogh's letters was the Hon. Robert R. Livingston who was minister to France at the time Louisiana was purchased from Napoleon, then First Consul. This magnificent domain was obtained in the spring of 1803 for $15,000,000 and added nine hundred thousand square miles of territory to our possessions. The Spaniards did not like this acquisition by the United States, and protested against the bargain. They raised vexatious questions as to the true boundaries of the territory, contending that they owned all the country east of the Mississippi. These limits were at length defined and the Spaniards were left in possession of the country along the Gulf of Mexico to the Atlantic Ocean, east of a line along the Pearl River, and south of the 31st parallel. This territory was known as West and East Florida. The Floridas were ceded to the United States, February 22d, 1819, in consideration of five million dollars, which however by the terms of the treaty was paid to American citizens in compensation for depredations committed by Spanish vessels.

The complicated questions arising from the varied claims of the French, the Spanish and the American governments and of private citizens are the subjects of discussion in Mr. McDonogh's letters, and, he says, "more than once commanded the attention of Daniel Webster and other great legal minds."

Next to education, the subject which appealed most strongly to the philanthropic heart of Mr. McDonogh was the liberation of his slaves, and, in general, the colonization of the colored man in Africa. His views are set forth at such length in the following letters that it will be unnecessary to elucidate them further than to speak of his relations to the American Colonization Society, and the results of his efforts as shown in the Liberian Republic. He was one of the founders of this society, of which Henry Clay was president, and for a long time Dr. Gurley was secretary; was one of the vice-presidents, a lifelong contributor to its funds, and at his death the society received by will from his estate the gift of one hundred thousand dollars.

The Republic of Liberia now includes a population of about two million persons, composed of the colonists, the civilized Christian natives, and the aborigines. It was founded by the American Colonization Society, which sent there from

America about eighteen thousand colored people. The colony declared itself an independent nation in 1847. Maryland, a negro republic to the east of Cape Palmas, founded as a colony in 1821 by philanthropists of Maryland, united with Liberia in 1857. The republic now embraces a territory of one hundred and fifty thousand square miles, and, if we may judge from the exhibit made at the World's Columbian Exposition, is a country rich in resources and products. It has not realized all the anticipations of the friends of colonization, but amid many difficulties has continued to grow steadily in spite of some attempts to destroy its independence made by the powers which are seeking empire in the Dark Continent.

The personal letters here published indicate a rare, old-fashioned courtesy and great felicity of expression. They also show the author to have been possessed of strong affections and a deeply religious nature. While he was inflexible in his theories of education and human responsibility, he was also loving and tender-hearted, delighting in children, music and flowers, and cherished to the last the deepest affection for his parents and other kindred.

RELATING TO THE LOUISIANA PURCHASE

PAPERS OF JOHN McDONOGH.

TO G. A. MAGRUDER, UNITED STATES SENATOR.

New Orleans, September, 1812.

Dear Sir:—

In fulfillment of my promise made to you when last I had the honor of seeing you, before your departure from this for the seat of government, I now beg leave to address you, enclosing you copies of the Title Deeds from the Spanish Government to lands sold me in that part of West Florida claimed and taken possession of by the Government of the United States, as forming a part of Louisiana under their purchase, which names are attached to and make part of this state, giving you at the same time, for your information, an account of such occurrences as took place under the Spanish government, as came to my knowledge relating to that district, and to the sales of land made in it, with such observations thereon as may strike me.

You will perceive, sir, by the enclosed title papers, the nature of the sales made in that district by the government of Spain, and continued by her up to the day on which the United States took possession of Baton Rouge, which, I believe, was in January, 1811 (the form and nature of all which sales are the same).

A valuable consideration in money was paid for them, as they were sold at a price, established by estimation, which was in many instances as high as 30, 35, and 40 cents per French arpent, (a measure less than the English acre,) which price, established in every instance by respectable estimators, appointed by the King on one side and by the purchasers on the other, assisted by the Surveyor General of Louisiana, added to the fees of office, Surveyor's fees, which are very heavy, and expenses of running, marking and bounding the lands, made them stand the purchasers, all expenses paid, in many instances as high as 60 to 75 cents per arpent.

You will also, sir, please find enclosed a certified copy of two royal orders of the King of Spain at Madrid to his Intendant, John Ventura Morales, whereby he ratifies all the acts of sales of land made by said Intendant up to their date, and instructs them to go on selling the royal lands in the manner most advantageous for the interest of his sovereign. Than the whole of those papers none can be more full and conclusive in the establishment of title.

The whole quantity of lands sold by the Spanish government in that district is of trifling amount, of no consequence to the government of the United States, and beneath its consideration. I assure you, and vouch to you, sir, for the truth of my assertion, that the whole quantity sold does not exceed half a million of arpents, and that divided amongst a great number of individuals and families, as it was sold by the government of Spain in tracts of every size, according to the abilities of the purchasers, from 2,000 arpents, 3,000, 5,000, 10,000, up to 50,000 and 100,000 arpents, and which lands, (now held in possession of the purchasers, in many instances, for ten years last past within a few months,) have passed through the hands of various purchasers for valuable considerations, in many instances have descended in succession, and in others have been seized, executed, and sold under decrees of courts of justice.

The people, sir, of that part of Florida are very unpleasantly situated, and are generally in a dissatisfied state, arising from this uncertainty in which their land titles are placed. This dissatisfaction is increased from their perceiving that no direct law, as yet, has been passed by Congress confirming all claims of individual and Spanish grants. A law of that nature they confidently expected would have been passed by Congress immediately after taking possession of their country. Since that period, two years now nearly they find have passed away, and they are still left in the same state of uncertainty; and from the late law of Congress establishing an office for the en-registering of doing, they perceive that that state of uncertainty is still likely to exist for several years; during which time of uncertainty their property must lie dead, as it can have no value, nor can acquire any, until the decision of the United States thereon.

I assure, you, sir, the situation of those people is particularly hard, and of sufficient interest to demand the immediate attention of the government. The population of that district, as you are no doubt well informed, is composed of French, Spanish, and Americans. The settlements of the A'rnite, Camite, and Tickfoha rivers are large and principally Spanish, but all American in heart. The people of that district for many years back were anxious to form a part of the American Confederacy. They made a struggle to that effect and succeeded therein.

They place every confidence in the justice of their government, and are convinced that nothing more is waiting than a proper representation of their claims, to have them at once confirmed. They therefore, sir, look forward to you, knowing your zeal for their interest, and your knowledge of their land claims, to have those claims laid before Congress, and a law passed at the ensuing session confirming all acts of the Spanish government up to the day on which the United States took possession of Baton Rouge, in January 1811.

For, sir, should such a law not be enacted, and our government attempt to lay aside or annul any acts of the late government, they thereby open a door to litigation which would not be closed in half a century. And that without any benefit to the general government, but on the contrary an injury. They would ruin many of the inhabitants, render them unhappy, dissatisfied, and ill disposed towards that government on whose success their claims depended, and that without any advantage, as I before observed, to the general government.

For should it set aside any of the Spanish titles, the old British titles would consequently come in and stand good, and on every foot of land sold by the Spanish government, and a great deal more, there is a British title and patent in existence, so that the general government would not gain a foot of land by setting aside any of the Spanish titles. In that event they would only deprive American citizens of them, to bestow them upon British subjects.

The general government, sir, having given to the inhabitants of that part of Louisiana which they first took possession of, a proof of their justice and liberality, it appears to me, in having so done, have thereby fixed and established a precedent, which they cannot get over, and which justice equally demands from them in the present instance. I allude, sir, to their having ratified all acts of the former government of this country up to the day on which they received possession of a part of it, which was on the 20th day of December, 1803.

They did, sir, even more. They confirmed to all claimants, as far as two thousand acres, even where no species of title existed, but where only a settlement had been made. How much more strong, sir, then, are the claims in the present instance, where a valuable consideration has been paid, and titles exist in complete forms, stamped by every necessary formality of the government, and even confirmed and ratified in the most solemn manner by the sovereign.

The purchase of Louisiana was made at Paris, on the 30th day of April, 1803, and the United States government ratified all acts of the former government up to the 20th day of December of the same year, the day on which they took possession of a part of it.

Now, sir, I would ask, if they ratified all acts of the late government up to the day on which they received a part of the country, would not justice and liberal policy point out the propriety of confirming in some manner all acts of the late government up to the day on which they took forcible possession of the remaining part, (I am wrong—not the remaining part, because the Mobile part claimed by the United States is still held by Spain,) which had been withheld and which is still a subject of contestation and negotiation between those governments?

I think it will, and I cannot, nor will not, doubt the justice of my country. Should the government not do so, one portion of the people will have just cause to complain that they are treated with less liberality by the government than another has been, and that a principle has been laid down for them different from that established for another portion of their fellow-citizens in an adjoining district.

Another case, sir, (which occurred between our government and that of Spain,) to which I beg leave to call your attention, in which the government of the United States have also established a precedent, as it appears to me decidedly in point, and which they cannot but acknowledge, is that where Natchez and a part of the Mississippi Territory were held for many years by Spain, but claimed by the United States. While held by her, she sold and gave away the lands by a thousand different grants, all of which grants, with all the acts of the Spanish government, (by an act as late as July of the present year, in a paper at the last session of Congress, to which I refer you,) have been ratified and confirmed by the government of the United States, up to the day on which they obtained possession.

Notwithstanding that it has been fully proven at the running of the line of demarcation by Elliot, and by the delivery of the country in dispute, afterwards, by Spain to the United States, that she, Spain, had committed acts of sovereignty over a country which did not belong to her, and to inflict which she had no pretensions, the government of the United States, in its justice, not being willing that individuals should suffer by the acts of a sovereign power whilst that power held the country, and it remained in dispute, a subject of contention, confirmed all the acts of the government of Spain.

And I perceive with much pleasure that this decided and wise policy of our government is consonant to, and coincides with, the doctrine laid down by all the celebrated writers on public law; who set forth that individuals should never be made to suffer loss under an act of a government where a country or territory was in dispute as to boundary—all acts of the government in possession, where individuals were concerned, being valid and obligatory on the government claiming and establishing its pretensions, the governments having their reasons for indemnity against one another, not against individuals.

I will now, sir, intrude still further upon your time, and prove to you, and to the government, that neither France nor

Spain ever considered the Baton Rouge district as forming a part of Louisiana, as retroceded by Spain to France.

Spain never contemplated giving it up to France, as forming a part thereof, as she had given orders in respect to that district long before the United States became a party in that transaction by purchasing from France; nor did France claim or expect to receive it. On the contrary, she acknowledged she had no claim to it under the treaty of St. Ildefonso, by which she acquired Louisiana from Spain, she only expecting to receive, in virtue of a retrocession from Spain, that which she had formerly delivered to her under a cession.

The government of Spain, on the 15th of October, 1802, expecting France to take possession of Louisiana (according to the treaty of St. Ildefonso), gave orders in consequence to her officers here for the delivery of the country, and instructed them to issue a proclamation to the inhabitants, inviting them to remove with the government into the district of Baton Rouge, offering them every facility, with grants of land, etc., etc.

A proclamation to that effect was issued by the Marquis Cassacalvo and the Governor Salceda, on the 18th day of May, 1803, inviting all Spanish subjects to remove into the Baton Rouge district, promising all those attached to the government land grants, and offering, to every one who wished to purchase, lands in the city of New Orleans, only eighteen days after the treaty was made in Paris for the purchase of Louisiana between France and the United States of America.

Consequently that event could not have been known, either here or in Spain in Europe, at that period. Even in Paris it was not known, being kept secret by consent of both parties until its ratification by the American government should have taken place.

This document, sir, is proof positive of the intention of Spain not to have given up Baton Rouge to France, that district not being included in the retrocession made to her of Louisiana, Spain not having received it from her on the cession of that country to her by France.

The order of the King of Spain to the Marquis Someruelos, dated Barcelona, 15th of October, 1802, for the delivering of Louisiana to France, is in these words:

"Charles, by the grace of God, King, &c., &c., having thought proper to retrocede to the French Republic the colony and province of Louisiana, I hereby order you immediately on your receipt of this, by the General Victor, or any other officer of that Republic duly authorized, to deliver up and put him in possession of Louisiana and its dependencies, as also the town and island of New Orleans, with the same extent which it actually has, and which it had when held by France when ceded to my Royal Crown, &c., &c." Signed by Me, the King, and countersigned, Pedri Cevallos, and the proclamation court of Spain appointed by the Marquis Someruelos for the delivering of Louisiana to France. Promulgated on the 18th day of May, 1803, in the city of New Orleans; actually defines its limits on the east; the Manshack, or Iberville, the American line, would remain in the possession of Spain, (it not forming a part of Louisiana,) in which districts Spanish subjects were invited to remove from Louisiana, &c., &c.

Another most important document, sir, (and which is proof conclusive that Spain delivered to France, in entire fulfillment of the treaty of St. Ildefonso, all the territory which she held a right to, and which France claimed as making part of Louisiana and to her full satisfaction acknowledged by her,) is the Process Verbal, made in the city of New Orleans on the 30th day of November, 1803, on the retaking of possession of Louisiana by France, in virtue of the treaty of St. Ildefonso, signed and acknowledged by the different commissioners of France and Spain: by the citizen Laussat, colonial Prefect, on the part of the Republic, and by the Marquis Cassicalvo and the Governor Salceda, on the part of Spain.

This document sets forth (after an exchange of powers, between the commissioners, &c., &c.): "That the said Marquis Cassacalvo, and Don M. Salcedo, do thereby declare that in virtue of the orders of the King of Spain, dated at Barcelona, on the 15th day of October, 1802, and countersigned by His Excellency Don Pedro Cevallos, principal secretary, counsellor of state for the delivering of Louisiana, and in entire fulfillment thereof, they now deliver to, and place from this moment, the said commissioner of France, the said Laussat, in possession of the colony and province of Louisiana and its dependencies, as also of the town and island of New Orleans, with the extent which it now actually possesses and such as it had in the hands of France as ceded to the Royal Crown of Spain, &c., &c."

I now beg leave to refer you, sir, to the treaty of Paris of the 30th of April, 1803, by which the United States acquired a title to and obtained possession of Louisiana:

"Article 1. Whereas, by the third article of the treaty concluded at Saint Ildefonso, on the first day of October, 1800, between the First Consul and his Catholic Majesty, it is connected as follows: His Catholic Majesty promises and engages on his side to retrocede to the French Republic, six months after the entire and full execution of the conditions and stipulations as following relative to the Duke of Parma, the Colony and Province of Louisiana, with the same extent which it at present has in the hands of Spain, and which it had when possessed by France, &c., &c. The First Consul, desirous of giving to the United States a proof of his friendship, cedes, in the name of the French Republic, in virtue of the aforesaid treaty, concluded with his Catholic Majesty, &c., &c."

Permit me now, sir, to ask you if any treaties, any state papers or documents, could be more clear and explicit, every one of them containing and repeating the same expressions, than the order of the King of Spain for the delivery of the country to France, the proclamation of the commissioners of Spain to the inhabitants of Louisiana, and the Process Verbal drawn up by the different commissioners of France and Spain?

Nothing. No papers can be more clear, more full, more conclusive. They are proof, demonstrative, of the understanding and construction put on the different treaties made between France and Spain relative to the limits of Louisiana on the east by those powers.

It was in consequence, sir, of that proclamation, issued, as I have before stated to you, by the commissioners of Spain for the delivery of Louisiana to France, in the city of New Orleans and on the 18th day of May, 1803, (which proclamation is, no doubt, in the archives of the government here, a copy of which I will procure and forward you,) that purchase of land was made of the Spanish government in the district; no suspicion existing, that the government of the United States had or could have any claims on that country as forming a part of Louisiana included in their purchase by the treaty of Paris on the 30th of April, 1803.

It would be, sir, a most unpleasant event, and one which I hope we may never be obliged to resort to, for the claimants of those lands, American citizens, to be obliged to contest their rights against the government of the United States, but which they would do to the end of time if forced to it.

That district is still a matter of discussion and negotiation between the three governments. The United States is one of three parties in the transaction; one of four parties, I may say, as Great Britian, the ally and guarantee of Spain, of consequence becomes a party; which government has already formally entered the protest of the Prince Regent to the act of taking possession of that district by our government.

France and Spain deny the claims of the United States. But in the meantime our government has taken possession of a part of the territory in dispute, not the whole. Therefore, as the case stands, there are two parties against one ; and we have lately seen, only a month since, the Governor of Pensacola, by the orders of his government, send and demand of Governor Clayborne that Baton Rouge and the part of Florida held by our government be immediately delivered up to the Spanish government, stating that in case of refusal his orders would oblige him to take it by force.

I would ask you, sir, in an attempt of that kind, whether it would not be of the first importance that the inhabitants of that district should be satisfied and attached to the government of the United States, ready and willing to turn out and defend it. You will recollect, sir, that the whole of that district is much exposed. It is the frontier of our state, with an extensive seaboard, the whole of which is open to an invading enemy, and contains, between the Mississippi and the Perdido, a bold and hardy militia, amounting to at least six thousand in number able to carry arms.

The claim of the United States, I am fearful, sir, from the view I have taken of the subject, cannot be supported against Spain. The government of the United States, by the construction they put on the treaty by which they acquired Louisiana from France, claims that district as far east as the river Perdido as being a part of Louisiana included in that purchase. Whether, sir, by that treaty, the government of the United States acquired a title to that district from France, or not, I shall not presume to determine. But I would ask you, if France has sold a territory to which she had no right or title, to the United States, does that give the United States a just right to it? Certainly not.

Having now, I presume, sir, satisfied you, by the foregoing

statement of facts and proofs, that neither France nor Spain ever considered the country lying between the American line and Iberville, and the lakes Maurepa and Pontchartrain, and the rivers Mississippi and Perdido, as forming a part of Louisiana, I will now go on to prove to your entire satisfaction, I trust, that our country never was part of Louisiana; that at all times (prior to the definitive and general treaty of peace of Paris of 1763, by which that country was confirmed to Great Britian) it was claimed by Great Britian as being part of her North America possessions on the Mississippi.

The lines between the territories of Great Britian and Louisiana belonging to France never had been established by treaty, and had been at all times a subject of misunderstanding and dispute between the two countries. France claimed all the country on the left side of the river, under the title of Louisiana, and England claimed as belonging to her, all the country on the left bank of the river Mississippi, excepting only the island of New Orleans.

Finally, that country, as claimed by Great Britian, was acknowledged by the court of France to belong to Great Britian. In consequence, it was left in her possession, and confirmed to her by treaty, under lines laid down and fully expressed, which forever established the boundaries of Louisiana and the territories of Great Britian on the Mississippi.

In proof, sir, of what I have asserted, I beg leave to take you back to the year 1761, and remind you of the war carried on at that time, with so much violence, in America as well as in Europe, between France and Great Britian. In the course of that year a proposal for peace was made by the court of France through the mediation of the Spanish monarch, which was favorably received by Great Britian; in consequence a minister at each court was appointed to carry on the negotiations.

On the 15th of July of that year, after various propositions had been received on each side, the court of France handed in a memorial to that of Great Britian, wherein, amongst other propositions which she makes as a basis for a definitive treaty of peace, is the following : "That the limits of Canada and Louisiana should be ascertained in such manner as to preclude all possibility of disputes on this subject after peace should be re-established."

Several additional proposals were made on each side, when France gave in her ultimatum to the proposals of Great Britian, which was answered the latter end of August by the court of Great Britian, who transmitted to France final articles insisted on by her. The second of these articles is in the following words:

"Article 2. As for the line drawn from Rio Perdido, contained in a notification delivered by Monsieur De Bussy on the 18th day of August, concerning the limits of Louisiana, his Majesty cannot but reject such an unexpected proposal as altogether inadmissible on these two accounts :

"The said line, under color of fixing the limits of Louisiana, includes in that province extensive countries which, with the posts and forts that command them, the Marquis De Vandreuil hath surrendered by the most solemn capitulation to his Britannic Majesty under the definition of Canada. Consequently, however contentious the respective pretensions of the two crowns might have been before the war, particularly with respect to the course of the Ohio and the territory adjacent, all the contending titles are settled since the surrender of Canada.

"The line proposed for ascertaining the limits of Louisiana cannot be admitted, because it would comprehend, on the side of Carolina, very extensive countries and numerous nations, which have always been considered as under the protection of the King, a connection which his Majesty has no intention to renounce, though, for the benefit of peace, he might consent to leave the intermediate countries that are under the protection of Great Britian, more particularly those inhabited by the Cherokees, Creeks, Chickisaws, Choctaws, and other nations situated between the British Settlements and the Mississippi."

Those articles insisted on by the British government as the basis of the treaty, of which the foregoing was one, were replied to by a new memorial to the court of London, dated the 9th day of September. In this the French King accedes to the limits and bounds of Louisiana as laid down and insisted on by the English Monarch, in the following words:

"The first paragraph concerning the limits of Louisiana, contained in the second article of England's answer, is allowed by France. The second paragraph is neither just nor clearly expressed. It is proposed, therefore, that it shall be definitely explained in the following terms. The intermediate Indian nations situated between the Lakes and the Mississippi, within the line described, shall be neutral and independent, under the protection of the King of France, and those without the line, on the side of the English posessions, shall also be neutral and independent, under the protection of the King of England."

To this memorial, which was delivered to the British government on the 18th day of September, 1761, the British ministry made no reply. Their minister was called from Paris and the negotiation for peace was thus broken off.

I have now, I trust, sir, by the foregoing statement of facts, for the correctness of which I refer you to the third chapter, fifth book, fourth volume of Smollet's History of England, proved to you, as I before asserted, that the limits of Louisiana had long remained undefined and a source of misunderstanding and dispute between the crowns of Great Britian and France.

It now only remains for me to prove that the territory in dispute, lying between the Mississippi and Perdido rivers, and claimed by the United States as being a part of her purchase from France, never formed a part of Louisiana.

This I have already done in part, by the foregoing statement of claims and acknowledgments of the courts of Great Britian and France, establishing the fact that, Louisiana never having been defined, its limits were long a subject of dispute.

I will now complete the proof by referring you to the seventh article of the definitive treaty of peace, concluded at Paris on the tenth day of February, 1763. The basis of this treaty, it was agreed by the respective courts of France and Great Britian, should be taken from the proposals and correspondence which had taken place, in the course of the negotiations between the courts of France and Great Britian in the year 1761, between France, Great Britian, Spain and Portugal, which irrevocably and forever established the limits of Louisiana, and is in these words:

"Article 7th. In order to re-establish peace on solid and durable foundations, and to remove forever all subjects of dispute with regard to the limits of the British and French territories on the continent of America, it is agreed that, for the future, the confines between the dominions of his Britannic Majesty and those of his most Christian Majesty in that part of the world, shall be fixed irrevocably by a line drawn along the middle of the river Mississippi from its source to the river Iberville, and from thence, by a line drawn along the middle of this river and the lakes Maurepas and Pontchartrain to the sea, and for this purpose the most Christian King cedes in full right and guarantees to his Britannic Majesty the river and port of the Mobile, and everything which he possesses or ought to possess on the left side of the river Mississippi, except the town of New Orleans and the island on which it is situated, which shall remain to France, &c., &c."

Thus, sir, did the treaty of '63 give form and shape to

Louisiana, establishing forever its limits on the east by a defined line, as anterior to that period it was a country vague and undefined by lines or treaty, and consequently a subject of continual dispute between the contending crowns.

To elucidate the subject still further, and to place it in as plain a point of view as possible, I will presume, sir, a little longer on your time and attention.

On the third day of November, in the year 1762, France ceded to Spain, by a secret convention, the country of Louisiana, with the town and Island of New Orleans. This cession was not known in France until the year '64. In the treaty of '63, France, in speaking of Louisiana, mentions it as a province still belonging to her. At that time, the King, in his letter from Versailles, dated 21st April, 1764, to Monsieur D'Abadie, the governor of the province, instructs him that, having ceded to his brother of Spain the country of Louisiana, he thereby orders him to make the delivery thereof with the town and island of New Orleans.

Those documents, sir, alone, are proofs positive, if no others existed, of the limits of Louisiana. Louisiana was ceded to Spain in 1762; she obtained possession in 1764. Did she receive the Baton Rouge district? No, she did not. It was in possession and held in sovereignty at that time under an old claim as a part of her North America possessions, and confirmed to her as such by the treaty of 1763 by Great Britain.

Did Spain protest on her not receiving the Baton Rouge district? Did she claim it as a part of Louisiana ceded to her in 1762? Neither; she neither claimed it nor protested against its being held by Great Britain. On the contrary she was one of the contracting powers in the treaty of '63, which confirmed that country to Great Britain.

Spain afterwards acquired that country by right of conquest. Having declared war against Great Britain in the year

1779, Spain in that and the two succeeding years reduced under her dominions Natchez, Baton Rouge, Mobile, Pensacola, and St. Augustine, and at the peace of Versailles which followed the whole of east and west Florida was confirmed to her by treaty by Great Britain.

By the treaty of St. Ildefonso, Spain retroceded Louisiana to France such as she received it from her. The words of one treaty are cession of the other retrocession. Now, sir, what is the meaning attached to these words? Is retrocession the act of giving back or returning that which had been received? If so, I ask then, did Spain receive that district from France? I answer, no, she did not; consequently, France can have no title to Baton Rouge and that district, nor can the United States, claiming under a title derived from her. The title rests in Spain.

But if our government received a title from France to that district, she of course has a claim upon her for indemnification for selling to her that which was not hers, and to which she had no title. By the correspondence of our government with that of France on the subject of this claim, you will find, sir, that Monsieur Talleyrand informed our minister at Paris, that he was instructed to say that France never had received from Spain any title to Baton Rouge and that district, and of consequence never could have sold, and never intended to sell, to the United States that which was not hers and to which she received no right.

I repeat to you, sir, that the holders of those lands have been much injured by the claim of the government, keeping their rights in a state of suspense. They look with confidence to you, knowing your knowledge of the land claims of the country, and your zeal, proved on so many occasions, to have their rights established, at the ensuing Congress, by a law confirming all acts of the Spanish Government up to January

1811, at which time they took possession of Baton Rouge. And they trust that justice and a wise policy will second your exertions in their cause in the councils of the nation.

   I have the honor to be, sir,
    With the highest consideration,
     Respectfully, &c., &c.,
      JOHN McDONOGH.

P. S. I have the honor, sir, to observe still further in explanation of my title deeds from the Spanish Government, that the original grant to me of those lands, with the order of survey to the surveyor general of Louisiana was made and dated in the year 1803, and that the surveys were actually made and finished in that year, although, owing to the great mass and press of business, my title papers were not expedited and completed until 1804.

   Most respectfully, sir,
     J. McD.

Note. In proof of my assertion "That the government of the United States would not be benefited in setting aside Spanish titles in existence for a great proportion of the lands in both east and west Florida, but particularly in that part of west Florida claimed by the United States, which of consequence in that event would come in and stand good," I beg leave to add the testimony given on this head by Smollet, in his continuation of Hume's History of England, in the eighth chapter, fifth book, fourth volume, and 416th page of his work, to which I refer you :

"On the 21st of November, 1763, the commissioners for trade and plantations gave public notice that all the lands in the provinces of east and west Florida should be surveyed and laid out into townships not exceeding twenty thousand acres each. Those townships, or any portions of them, were to be granted to persons who were willing to enter into reasonable engagements to settle the lands within a limited time and at their own expense with a proper number of useful, industrious, Protestant inhabitants upon the same moderate conditions of quit rent and cultivation as are required in other colonies.

"The soil of those lands was adapted to the raising of silk, cotton, wine, oil, indigo, cochineal with the like commodities, and notwithstanding all the reports that had been propagated to their disadvantage, a vast number of families complied with the terms of the offer, and those provinces soon bade fair to be among the most flourishing belonging to the British dominions."

      I have the honor to be,
       Your humble servant,
The Hon. A. B. Magruder,   JOHN McDONOGH.
 Senator from the
  State of Louisiana.

TO HON. HENRY JOHNSON, MEMBER CONGRESS.

      New Orleans, January 14, 1819.
Dear Sir:—

I had the pleasure of addressing you on the 30th ult., since when I am without a line from you. Our legislature assembled on the 4th inst., and on the 11th elected Mr. James Brown to fill the vacancy occasioned by the expiration of the term of Mr. Froment in the Senate of the United States.

I will not say in what way his election was obtained.

His being elected was the surprise of every one. He has talents, but nothing is expected from his labors. No confidence is placed in him.

The report of the Secretary of the Treasury to Congress of a plan for the settlement of the land claims of Florida has not yet reached us. It is looked for with much anxiety. The history of the land claims of that district, you, sir, of course, are perfectly acquainted with. The memorial of the Louisiana legislature to Congress in 1817 having given a complete exposition of them, it is unnecessary for me to say more on the subject.

Information from a source entitled to confidence, and of the highest respectability, assured us several months since, that in the outlines of an arrangement for the settlement of all our differences with Spain, made at Washington in May last between the Executive and Don Onis, (which outlines were forwarded to Spain,) the government of the United States engaged by a special article to confirm all titles to land made by Spain in east and west Florida, to the dates of taking possession of the respective parts thereof by the United States, excepting only two or three grants, made lately by the court of Spain in east Florida to some Spanish noblemen, of nearly the whole of that province, which grants Spain contracted to annul.

And report says the only reason this arrangement was not acted on at Madrid, and followed by a treaty, was the arrival there at the same moment of the news of the taking of Pensacola by the American forces.

I make mention to you, sir, of this report, merely to say that, if true, notwithstanding that no treaty was based on the arrangement, the United States can never contest the land claims of Florida, nor reject a law to establish them, after having thus formally agreed to confirm them.

The Secretary of the Treasury, as one of the cabinet, was of course acquainted with the arrangement, if such a one took place, and I should be happy to learn from you, sir, the truth or incorrectness of this report.

Our state is much interested in the revival of some of the late laws of Congress, and in the passing of others, some few of which I will take the liberty of mentioning to you.

On the third of March, 1811, Congress passed a law giving to the front proprietors on water courses in Louisiana the right of purchasing to the extent of thirty arpents back of the tract owned by them, and limited the duration of the law, I think, to two years, within which term subscriptions were to be made, and pointed out the mode of appointing the officers who were to receive the subscriptions, &c., &c.

This law expired without ever having been carried into effect in this district. The office was never opened under it, the officers appointed never appeared, and no individual ever had it in his power to subscribe under it. Mr. Robertson was repeatedly informed of it, and he promised not only to have the law revived, but to do more, to have one passed containing the second depth as a donation. This the proprietors were certainly entitled to, as under the ancient government they had only to ask for it to obtain it.

But it appears he neglected it, for he neither did one nor the other. It is therefore, sir, highly important to revive this law, extending merely the time for subscribing, pointing out the mode of opening the office, appointing officers, &c. Congress cannot object to it, as the first never was carried into effect, and never was acted on; at least not in this district. Whether it was in the western district or not I cannot say.

The revival of this law forms also a part of the prayer of the memorial of the legislature of this state to Congress in 1817. The revival of the law for the enregistering of land claims throughout the state also formed a part of the prayer of said memorial, and is much desired, as a great many claims, as well in this district as in Florida, are yet unregistered, owing in a measure to the French and Spanish inhabitants being unacquainted with our language, and ignorant of the law relative to their land claims. Congress of course cannot hesitate to extend the term of enregistering six or twelve months longer.

In the bill introduced by Mr. Brown in the Senate of the United States two years since, for the settlement of the Florida land claims, (which was so generally deprecated throughout the state,) it was observed that it provided not only for the confirmation of all British titles, but for the incomplete French or Spanish titles to the extent of twelve hundred arpents only, whereas all former laws of the United States confirm, through every other part of Louisiana, the incomplete French or Spanish title to the extent of a league square.

It is therefore expected, in any law that may be passed in relation to the subject, that the claimants in Florida will be placed at least on a footing with those of the other parts of Louisiana.

No law has yet been enacted by Congress providing for the sale of public lands in this state. A hardy population on our western border is greatly to be desired. The safety and prosperity of the state indeed require it, and the sooner it is procured the better. But the only mode by which it can be accomplished is that of throwing the public lands into the market.

Why such a measure has been delayed so long has excited general surprise. It is one of primary importance to our state. I am aware, sir, that it is unnecessary to call your attention to the claims of those gentlemen who suffered by the British invasion in the late war, as you have already devoted yourself to the subject.

I will, therefore, only observe, that the greater part of the claims yet unliquidated, and particularly those of Governor Villere, Messrs. Jumonville, DeVilliers, Lacoste, Duverje, Lefebvre, &c., are of that description which come completely in the late law of Congress on the subject, and stand on the same footing with those which have been already paid.

I cannot but observe, whilst on the subject, that even as relates to those claims which have been already paid, a most extraordinary course has been pursued by the auditors at Washington. After having fulfilled, not only the letter, but the spirit of the law, in every respect, by commissioners here, noways interested, who took the necessary testimony, made estimations, &c., not a single claimant received the whole amount of his claim. Some were allowed three-fourths of the amount, some one-half, and many others but the one-fourth or one-fifth part of the amount of their claim.

On what principle the auditors acted, I cannot conceive. The claimants were entitled to the whole of their claims, justly substantiated under the law, or they were entitled to nothing. I am decidedly of the opinion that they have a just claim for, and should be paid the amounts deducted from, their several accounts.

I am pleased to find that the general government has made the slaves belonging to our citizens, carried away by the British at the evacuation of our state and after the conclusion of peace off our territory, a subject of reclamation and negotiation, under the treaty with that government.

The claim is a correct one, and no doubt will be met in a spirit of justice by the British government. At all events our citizens must be indemnified by our own, if they are not by the British government, as no claim can be more strongly founded in justice than theirs is.

Being perfectly acquainted with the nature of those claims,

having had a personal agency in relation to them, I will sketch you in a few lines their history, as, notwithstanding your acquaintance with it, there may be circumstances in relation to it of which you are not fully aware.

At the evacuation of the island of Orleans by the British army in 1815, the naval and military commanders of their forces carried away with them from the banks of the Mississippi to their rendezvous in Cat or Ship Island, I forget which, within our state, the slaves in question, the property of our fellow-citizens. These slaves were landed and detained on that island. The evacuation of the island of Orleans took place on the 19th of January of that year.

Somewhere about the 25th to the 30th of the same month, the commander-in-chief of our army, General Andrew Jackson, dispatched a flag of truce to the British fleet with three gentlemen, bearers of his dispatches, viz.: Edward Livingstone, his aid-de-camp, R. D. Shepherd, and W. White, Esqs., for the purpose of effecting an exchange of prisoners, as proposed by the British commanders, and of demanding the restoration of the slaves carried off.

Whilst these gentlemen were on board the fleet, a dispatch frigate arrived from England, bringing the British commanders official accounts of the conclusion of peace between the two governments, and they succeeded in all the objects of their mission. An arrangement took place for the exchange of prisoners, and the British commanders, both naval and military, assured these gentlemen that they were ready and willing to deliver the slaves, whenever their owners, or agents of the owners, would come to receive them.

They stated further, that it had not been their wish to have brought the slaves away, that they came away with them at the evacuation without their knowledge or consent, and they were anxious to get clear of them, and to deliver them to their owners; and they particularly requested those gentlemen to say to General Jackson, that if he would grant a flag of truce to their owners it should be respected and the slaves delivered to them, and that the fleet would not leave their then anchorage for a certain length of time (I think somewhere about a month from that day).

Those gentlemen at the same time saw and conversed with many of the slaves, who all expressed the strongest desire to return to their masters. On the return of those gentlemen from the British fleet they reported to General Jackson the result of their mission, and informed the gentlemen, owners of the slaves in question, of the acquiescence of the British commanders in their demands for the restitution of the slaves, and of their willingness to deliver them up, recommending them to see General Jackson immediately, obtain a flag of truce, and proceed without loss of time to the British fleet to receive them.

At this stage of the transaction I was called on by several of the gentlemen interested, to request, as they did not speak the English tongue, that I would be their organ in the interview with General Jackson, for the purpose of requesting of him the necessary passports and flag of truce to enable them to proceed to the British fleet to obtain their slaves.

I acceded to their request, and informed them that, previous to waiting on General Jackson, I would see the gentlemen who had just returned from the fleet, to be assured of the amount of the conversation held by them with the British commanders. Accordingly I saw, in company with Mr. Jumonville, Messrs. Shepherd and White, who repeated to me all I have above stated.

From the interview with those gentlemen, we proceeded to the headquarters of General Jackson, whom we found. There were several gentlemen with him, one of whom was Mr. Livingstone, his aid, just returned from the British fleet.

I opened the conversation with General Jackson by informing him that I waited on him as the organ of those gentlemen who had had their slaves carried off by the British, for the purpose of requesting passports and a flag of truce for them to proceed to the British fleet to obtain them; and finished by stating to him the willingness and desire of the British commanders to deliver them, as reported by the gentlemen of his own family, who had had a personal understanding with them on the subject.

To my surprise and astonishment General Jackson positively refused granting passports or a flag of truce, notwithstanding all I could urge to induce him, and my reiterated demand. The reason he gave for his refusal, and which he repeatedly asserted before the gentlemen present, was, that the interests of his country did not permit him to grant it.

As I asserted, sir, in the commencement, that no claims could be more strongly founded in justice than those are, and that the claimants must be indemnified by our own if they should not be so by the British government, I have gone into this exposition of them for the purpose of showing in what way a claim was acquired against our own government.

All governments are responsible for the acts of their officers. General Jackson, the commander-in-chief of this district, and at that time supreme dictator, as he had put down all other authority and declared martial law, declared that the interests of his country did not permit him to grant passports to the owners of those slaves to go and receive them.

They were consequently sacrificed to the general good for the safety of the whole, and the general government is of consequence responsible, and must indemnify their owners. Individuals in such a case cannot suffer a loss.

That the claim, however, is a valid one, and one that the British government is bound to meet under the treaty, and cannot avoid paying, there is no doubt. Proof can be adduced, by hundreds of individuals, that the slaves were taken away by the British fleet, from off the American territory, at a period four or five weeks subsequent to their having received the official account of peace between the two governments, and upwards of three months after the date of the treaty of Ghent.

For further elucidation of the subject, I refer you to papers left by S. H. Harper, Esq., as he informs me, in the hands of Messrs. Lee and Wallack, of Washington, and particularly to certificates of Messrs. Shepherd, White, and myself.

As the President of the United States and Congress appear to be at issue relative to the constitutionality of appropriating by law the public moneys for the carrying on of canals, &c., it may be premature to move the subject at this moment.

But as it appears to be the general opinion the question will be decided this session, and that Congress has that right, I will beg leave to observe, that should it be so decided, I trust and hope that Louisiana, having equal rights with the other states to be benefited thereby, will come in for a participation of the advantages.

There is no other state in the Union where greater benefit would be derived from their formation, and none where canals can be formed with such facility and ease, nature having done so much towards it in our favor.

For the present I will confine myself to the pointing out to you two lines on which canals can be formed, although several others of much importance can be shown, which would, if executed, be of the greatest value, not only to this but to the general government, and tend mostly to the benefit of our state.

One is about five miles from the city of New Orleans, on

the left bank of the Mississippi, to commence on the river and extend through the plantation of Governor Villere, a distance of three or four miles on a straight line, to communicate with the Bayou Bienvenu, which bayou falls into Lake Borgne and the sea to the east of the Mississippi.

This canal, already in part executed, could be accomplished at an expense of one hundred and fifty thousand dollars. Vessels could come through it into the Mississippi drawing seven to eight feet of water. They now come in its present state within that distance of the river, there being, I am told, never less than seven feet of water on the bar where it joins Lake Borgne.

By casting your eye on the map of Louisiana, you will at once see the situation of this bayou, and the advantages it offers in being opened, the bayou itself being a handsome river of a hundred and fifty to two hundred feet in width. The general government is greatly interested in opening this communication with the Mississippi, as through it they could introduce their armed vessels, gunboats, &c.

That the advantage which would be enjoyed from such a channel of communication is seen by the general government, I have only to observe, is proved by their having, many years since, appropriated twenty-five thousand dollars as a donation to the Navigation Company of this city, whenever they would extend the Carondelet Canal into the Mississippi, so as to give a free ingress and egress to their gunboats from Lake Pontchartrain.

But as that canal has but four feet of water, and never can have any more, owing to the depth of the lake, where the Bayou Saint John communicates with it, the company never will be able to take advantage of this appropriation in its favor.

Were the canal formed which I have just pointed out, not only would the general government be greatly benefited in relation to their marine, but it would be a source of great revenue, as through it the whole commerce with the Floridas would be carried on, as well as a great part of that with Cuba, the coasting trade of the Atlantic board, &c.

The second canal line to which I will draw your attention, should commence on the right bank of the Mississippi, immediately in front of the city of New Orleans, and, extending back about six miles, communicate with the Bayou Villar, a considerable stream which joins the river and Lake Barataria and communicates with the sea to the west of the Mississippi.

This canal is also in part executed, and could be completed at an expense of a hundred and fifty to two hundred thousand dollars, so as to bring vessels drawing six or eight feet of water through it into the Mississippi.

The general government is also much interested in opening this communication with the Mississippi from the sea to the westward for their armed vessels. It would also be a source of great revenue, as the whole of the commerce of the Gulf of Mexico would be carried on through it, as well as the internal commerce of the western counties of the state, the lower La Faniche, Attakapas, and Opelousas, as the whole of that part of the country is intersected by natural bayous communicating with one another.

There would then be a constant and regular intercourse throughout the year with those counties, whereas now there is no internal communication with them by water but for about four or five months during the high water of the Mississippi. For the residue of the year none of their produce can reach us except by sea.

On the decision of the question, should it be found, sir, that Congress has the constitutional right to carry on works of this nature, and you should determine to bring the subject forward in the Senate, I take the liberty of suggesting to you, (as the course no doubt would be that of naming gentlemen on the spot, men of science and knowledge, to survey the grounds over which it was contemplated to form the canals, and to report to the proper department their opinion of the practicability of forming them, the advantages to be derived from them, with an estimate of the expense, &c.,) the importance of not naming persons whose interests would be in opposition to the objects contemplated, and to insure the appointment of such persons only as are disinterested.

Any members of our community may be selected, except such as are interested in the navigation company, either as stockholders or directors. Their interests would, of course, be opposed to the opening of other canals, as it would take away from their revenue. At any time you may request it, I will forward you a list of the directors and stockholders of that institution.

The defences of our state will also, sir, require your attention. Much is to be said on that subject. Those begun have made but small progress; there is something wrong. Many of the workmen, I am told, desert for want of pay, as the government leaves its agent without money. If this is a fact, it is surprising indeed, when we reflect on the immense revenue of their customs here.

I shall have the pleasure of addressing you again in a few days, sir, on other topics interesting to our state, as the present letter has already exceeded the length I had prescribed to myself.

With great respect, I have the honor to be, sir,
Your most obedient and humble servant,
JOHN McDONOGH.

TO THE HON. GEORGE A. MAGRUDER.

New Orleans, December, 1831.

Dear Sir:

The last time I had the pleasure of seeing you here, previous to your departure for Washington, you requested me to give you the history of the Florida land claims.

This I should have done; but I was informed by our friend McFalsh, who is perfectly correct, a day or two thereafter, that he had given you a note in relation to them, and had referred you particularly to the report of the case of Foster and David Nelson, decided in the Supreme Court of the United States, where its history is so fully explained that I consider anything further quite unnecessary.

I will therefore, sir, merely observe in relation to them, that those titles are not common grants or concessions made to settlers, but purchases for valuable consideration, made in the years 1803, 1804, and 1805, of the government of Spain; that the title went through all the forms of the social government of the country, were surveyed at great expense, and were sent to Spain, where they were confirmed by the king in council.

Than those titles none are stamped with greater solemnity of character and form. And, to wind up, they were ratified and confirmed by the government of the United States itself, under the 8th article of the treaty with Spain in 1819. It is unnecessary for me to say to you, sir, that the claimants here place all their hopes and confidence in you and in your exertions in their favor.

Should the President recommend the subject in his message to Congress, the course to be taken will be a plain one. Should he not do so, it will be necessary to introduce a bill on the subject, or have a committee appointed to investigate, report, &c, &c.

Whatever course may be taken, we beg of you to commence it without a moment's loss of time, otherwise it would not be gotten through the present session, notwithstanding it is the long one.

We take the liberty of requesting you to advise with Mr. Livingston on the course to be pursued, as he is perfectly acquainted with the natnre and justice of those claims, and he will aid you by all the means in his power. The President, perhaps, may be induced to forward a special message to Congress on the subject. Mr. Livingston, in a late communication, assured us it should be brought before Congress in such a way as to bring, he doubted not, a favorable result.

The claimants propose, as you are aware, that Congress shall confirm our title to the residue of the land on each tract, after deducting the quantity which the settlers are confirmed in, and indemnify us for the quantities taken from us by the settlers, by permitting us to locate equal quantities on other public lands within the state of Louisiana.

The Honorable Mr. Webster, of the Senate, we have no doubt, will assist you in every way in his power, perfectly acquainted as he is with the subject, as he was counsel for the claimants in the case of Foster and David Nelson; as will also our friend Isaiah S. Johnston.

I shall be happy, sir, to hear from you, and will thank you to forward me the report of the Secretary and Treasurer to Congress as soon as published. Command me at all times without ceremony, and believe me to be,

   With great respect and regard,
    Your most obedient and humble servant,
      JOHN McDONOGH.

CONCERNING

THE LIBERATION OF HIS SLAVES

AND

THE COLONIZATION OF LIBERIA

MR. McDONOGH'S LETTER
RELATING TO THE FREEING OF HIS SLAVES.

[Addressed to the New Orleans Commercial Bulletin.]

McDonogh, opposite New Orleans,
July 10th, 1842.

Messrs. Editors,

In a piece written by me in June last, on the subject of sending away some of my black people to Africa, and published

---

Note.—In addition to the value which attaches to this paper on account of its discussion of the problem of emancipation, once so vital, but now happily no longer a living issue, this experiment of Mr. McDonogh possesses extraordinary interest for all students of social science.

The principles of human nature are essentially the same in all races and conditions. What Mr. McDonogh says in regard to the relation of hope to the promotion of industry, thrift and morality, is of profound importance; nor would it be difficult for those who consider and discuss the relations of employer and employee, of capital and labor, to find in this letter suggestions of the utmost value in the remarks regarding the necessity of mutual confidence and respect.

This remarkable letter has never been referred to as a valuable contribution to social ethics, but it is respectfully commended to the consideration of the philosophers who are grappling with the problems of society. Would not the application of the same principles which resulted in giving these black men their freedom, contribute in many cases to emancipate men from the slavery of idleness and poverty?

in your paper the 24th of that month, I observed "that the act of sending those people away is, in my case, one of simple honesty alone. I lay no claim, nor am I entitled, to any credit or praise on the score of generosity.

"My meaning in the above assertion I will explain, Messrs. Editors, through your paper, should my leisure admit of it, at some future time, and the rather, as it may perhaps be of service to the slaveholders of the state, to know how one who has had much to do for the past forty years with the treatment of slaves has succeeded in it.

"When they find, from my experience, that they can send their whole gangs to Africa, every fifteen years, without the cost of a dollar to themselves, what master will refuse to do so much good, when it will cost him nothing in the doing, and afford him at the same time such high gratification, in knowing that he has contributed to making many human beings happy?

"For my experience will show, that, with a proper treatment of slaves, the gain from their extra labor, that is, the labor over and above that which slaves in general yield their owners, in the course of that time, say fifteen years, will enable their master to send them out, and purchase in Virginia or Maryland, with the gain made from said extra labor, a gang of equal number to replace them.

"In addition to which, what an amount of satisfaction, I would ask every humane master, would he not enjoy, in knowing that he was surrounded by friends, on whose faithfulness and fidelity he and his family could rely, under every possible contingency!

In fulfillment of said promise, I now undertake to explain the observation I then made, "that the act of sending those people is in my case one of simple honesty alone," and to show the mode I pursued, after much experience and reflection on the subject, for many years, in their treatment, and its results.

Before commencing, however, this long detail of treatment, and its attending circumstances, I will premise, to those who feel an interest in the subject and will take the trouble to read this recital, that it is one of egotism throughout. It tells of what the master said and what he did, from the beginning of the chapter to its end. In this, therefore, I shall be excused. It is what I promised, and there is but one way of telling the story to make it intelligible.

To proceed then and give you the plan that I laid down for myself, and have pursued for the last seventeen years, for the conduct and management of those I held in bondage, I have to observe, that, having at all times been opposed to laboring on the Sabbath day, except in cases of actual necessity, one of my rules for their walk and guidance in life always was, that they should never work on that holy day, prohibited as we were from so doing by the Divine law.

A long experience, however, convinced me of the impossibility of carrying it out in practice by men held in bondage, and obliged to labor for their master six days in the week; and I saw, on reflection, much to extenuate as to them the offense agains my rule. They were men, and stood in need of many little necessaries of life, not supplied by their master, and which they could obtain in no other way but by laboring on that day.

I had therefore often to shut my eyes and not see the offense, though I knew my instructions on that head were not obeyed; and in consequence, after long and fruitless exertions, continued for many years, to obtain obedience to that injunction, I determined to allow them the one-half of Saturday, say Saturday from midday until night, to labor for themselves, under a penalty, well understood by them, of punishment for disobedience, if they violated thereafter the Sabbath day, and sale to some other master.

From this time, which was about the year 1822, the Sabbath day was kept holy. Church was regularly attended, forenoon and afternoon; for I had a church built expressly for them on my own plantation, in which a pious neighbor occasionally preached on the Sabbath day, assisted by two or three of my own male slaves, who understood, preached, and expounded the Scriptures passably well; and at times I read them a sermon myself.

I perceived in a very short time a remarkable change in their manners, conduct, and life, in every respect for the better. We proceeded in this way, happy, prosperous, and blessed in every respect by the Most High, for about three years, or until 1825.

They in general labored for myself, though permitted to labor for whom they pleased, giving the preference to their master, even at a less rate of wages, on whose honesty they could depend for payment; for they were paid as regularly as the night came.

In the long days of summer, I paid the men for their Saturday afternoon labor at the rate of sixty-two and a half cents per day, the women at the rate of fifty cents per day. In the short days of winter, I paid the men at the rate of fifty cents per day, the women thirty-seven and a half cents per day, and the larger boys and girls in proportion.

Seeing the amount of money which they gained by their Saturday afternoon labor, I was led to calculate in what length of time, by labor, economy, and perseverance in well-doing, they would be able to purchase the remaining five and a half days of the week, seeing they had a capital of their own, and by that means obtain freedom for themselves and their children.

In this calculation I soon satisfied myself that it could be effected in the space of fourteen or fifteen years at the farthest. The next consideration with me was, "Is it my interest to assist them in its accomplishment, or can I, by any means I can devise, make it become my interest to assist them to obtain their freedom in this time?"

This also required reflection and calculation. I went at it, and in a very short time, from the clearest of all deductions, was convinced and satisfied that it could be done; and that it was in every point of view that the subject could be looked at and considered, to my interest; more especially when I took into view the considerations of satisfaction, pleasure, and happiness, which I should enjoy in promoting the happiness of others.

When thus satisfied that the project was good in itself, and worthy of trial for various solid reasons, I determined to lay my plan before them, and explain it in all its bearings; that is, before some ten or twelve men and women—those men and women in whom the others had confidence, and to whom they looked up at all times, for their superior talents, capacities, and virtues, for counsel and advice.

For it is the same with the black as with the white man. Assemble together for the first time twenty or fifteen white men, a company of soldiers, for instance, and within forty-eight hours after being brought together, though strangers to each other, the great majority will place their eyes on certain men among them, for their wisdom, courage, and virtue, to whom they, unknowingly to one another, determine to look up, as leaders or chiefs, to conduct, counsel, and advise them.

This I did when church service was over, on a Sabbath afternoon; observing to them, that, having their welfare and happiness, in this world as well as in the next, very much at heart, I was in consequence greatly desirous of serving them and their children; that in furtherance of these views and desires, I had a plan to propose to them:

"If you have confidence in the truth and honesty of your

master, of his friendship to you, and sincere desire to serve you and do you good, I have a plan to propose. Except you have that confidence in him, and regard, friendship and esteem for him, there will be no use in saying a word more about it, or in attempting to carry out the plan I have to propose to you. For I notify you beforehand, it cannot succeed if the most unlimited confidence and esteem do not exist, as well as on the side of the master as of the servant.

"This will from this day change the whole course of your lives, though I acknowledge, in justice to all, that I have no particular charge to make against the morality of your past lives and walk in love and fear of God.

"If you and your children will be faithful, honest, true, sober, economical, industrious, not eye servants, laboring night and day, considering the affairs and interests of your master as the affairs, concerns, and interests of each and every one of you individually, and all this with a fixed determination to persevere in well-doing to the end, under every temptation that may assail you, and over every obstacle that may fall in your way, and will in everything be ruled, directed, and guided by me, I will then, in that case, and under this full agreement and understanding between us, undertake so to manage your affairs, by becoming your banker, the keeper of your gains, and of your accounts, as to assure your freedom, and that of your children, with the blessings of the Most High.

"That is, your freedom in Liberia, the land of your fathers, a great and glorious land. For let it be understood between us, it is your freedom in Liberia that I contract for. I would never consent to give freedom to a single individual among you, to remain on the same soil as the white man. You can gain your freedom within the term, according to my estimate and calculation, of fifteen or sixteen years, or thereabouts, say a year or two sooner, or a year or two later. This will be effected in conformity with my plan and estimate, in the following way.

The one-half of Saturday being already your own, in consequence of my agreement with you that no work should be done on the Sabbath day, your first object will be to gain a sufficient sum of money to purchase the other half of Saturday, which is one-eleventh part of the time you have to labor for your master, and of consequence the one-eleventh part of the value your master has put upon you, and which you have to pay him for your freedom.

"This, I notify you, will be the most difficult part of your undertaking, and will take the longest time to accomplish. It is to be effected by laboring for me on Saturday afternoons, and leaving the amount of your labor in my hands to be husbanded for you. By foregoing everything yourselves, and drawing as little money as possible out of my hands, I calculate you will be able to accomplish it in about seven years.

"That once accomplished, and one day out of six your own, you will go on more easily and rapidly. Indeed, that once effected, your success is certain. Proceeding then in your good work, you will be enabled easily, by your earnings on one entire day in each week, to effect the purchase of another day of your time, in about four years.

"Now, master and owner of two days in each week, you will be able in two years more to purchase another day, so that three days, or the one half of your time, will be your own. In one and a half years more, you will be able to purchase another day, making four days your own; in one year more, another, or the fifth day; and in six months, the last day, or the whole of your time, will be your own.

"Your gains in less than one year, added to what the youths have gained in the meantime, will suffice to free your children, and all will be accomplished.

"In the foregoing estimate I calculate that you will draw

from me, occasionally, some small sums of money to furnish such little necessaries as you may need. But you must remember that when one draws, the whole of you, each individual, must draw at the same time ; the men an equal part each, the women the three-fourths part each of the sum drawn by the men.

"That you may be estimated at fair and reasonable prices —say the men at six hundred dollars each, the women at four hundred and fifty, and the boys, girls, and children in proportion—an account shall be made at once in my books, and your valuations charged.

"No account will be taken of the increased values of the youth and children as they advance in age, and no child will be charged that shall be born after the commencement of this agreement. This is in some measure a counterbalance to an interest account, as none will be calculated or allowed you on the amount of your gains in my hands.

"Such men and women as have no children of their own, when they have worked out their prices, shall be held and obliged to work and assist in paying for the children of others, so that the whole company shall go on the same day on board ship, and sail for your fatherland.

"I expect, and shall insist on, strict performance of your moral and religious duties in every respect, and church regularly attended by you and your children, forenoon and afternoon, on the Sabbath day.

"I would not agree to keep an immoral or bad servant, or one who would be obliged to be chastised for offenses, on any consideration. Should any of you therefore commit crimes at any time, while serving under this agreement, he or she will be immediately put up at public sale, (their offenses declared and made known,) and sold; and whatever money they had earned under this agreement shall go to the benefit of the others in general."

I have now to state, that during the whole of the period that they were laboring for themselves, I had to sell, for conduct I could not pardon, but two individuals. This should not be considered strange, looking at the situation in which they were placed, in the vicinage of such a city as New Orleans, and oftentimes within its bosom for months together.

Their surprise and astonishment at such a proposal, coming, as it did, from a master who had unlimited power over them and their time, they expecting nothing of the kind, may easily be conceived. They gave their consent with tears of joy, declared the confidence they entertained of my truth, honesty, and pure intentions to do them and their children good, and their willingness and determination to be guided in all things by me, and to make my will and my interest, after the Divine will, the study and rule of their lives.

On separating, I told them to communicate my plan and proposals to their adult fellow servants, male and female, and to say to them, none were bound to come into the agreement who had any objection to it—that such as did not wish to accept it, should go under the old regulations.

And I requested one and all of them to consult together through the week, and to give me their final answer and determination on the next Sabbath in church, when it should be confirmed or abandoned.

At the same time I charged them, as they valued my affection, to keep what I had said to them (desirous as I was to avoid, by so doing, the making of the slaves on other plantations unhappy or discontented) in their own bosoms, and never to disclose it, until after they should have left for Africa, to a living being on earth. "Be content," said I to them, "with the good you are about to receive, and keep the knowledge of it to yourselves." This they promised me they would do, and I believe they religiously did.

On the next Sabbath, I met them in church, and was told they had informed all their fellow servants of my views and intentions toward them, that they had well reflected during the past week on all that I had said to them, that they were at a loss for words to express their love and gratitude to me for what I had done and was now desirous of doing for them and their children; that they had always looked on me in the light of a father, deeply interested in their welfare, and that I was the only true friend they had on earth.

They said further that they had accepted one and all the proposals I had made them, and were determined, with the assistance of the Most High, to make a change in life; to live and walk in the Divine law; to be guided, in all worldly conduct, implicitly by my directions and counsel, and to fulfill with all the energy of their souls the agreement they had entered into with me. On this I observed to them that it was all well; that the agreement and contract were concluded; that we would, on both sides, master and servants, begin from that day to execute and carry it out, and that I would put down in handwriting all that I had said to them, that no mistakes might arise thereafter as to what I had said or what I had not said.

"To put you, however, more fully in possession of my scheme for your benefit, to give you a more perfect understanding of the contract which you are about to take on yourselves, so that in the carrying of it out complete success may attend it on both sides, and neither party, master nor slave, may be disappointed, I will inform you what I expect to realize, and how it is to be effected.

"My object is your freedom and happiness in Liberia, without loss of a cent to myself from sending you away and conferring that boon, as the humble instrument of the Most High, on you and your children. How, you naturally inquire, is that to be done? I will tell you how it is to be done.

"There is but one way, one mode to effect it, that I can see, or devise, and that is by greater assiduity and exertions in the slave to his labor during the usual hours of day labor, and especially by extra hours of labor before day in the morning, and after night in the evening.

"One hour after night in the evening, and one hour before day in the morning, would be two hours extra in twenty-four hours, which would be the one-sixth part more time devoted to labor than is generally demanded of the slave. This is equivalent to two years and a half of additional labor in fifteen years.

"Two hours extra labor before day in the morning, and two hours after night in the evening, would be four hours extra in every twenty-four hours, which would be the one-third part more of time devoted to labor than is generally demanded of the slave. This would be equivalent to five years of additional and extra labor in fifteen years.

"Without a scheme of this kind," said I to them, "by means of which you can effect a greater amount of labor in a given time than you could otherwise do, I could not afford to send you out. Without it, my sending you to Liberia, under the agreement, and in the mode I propose of permitting you to gain your freedom by laboring during the time that belongs to your master, and by that means paying him for your time, though it appears specious in itself, would be, in reality, making you a present of your time—making you and your children a gift of your freedom.

"For as the whole of your time belongs to your master, (the Sabbath day excepted, on which holy day neither master nor servant is permitted to labor,) if he was to permit you to work on a certain part of it, to make money to purchase your freedom, he would, in reality, in so doing, make you a gift of your freedom, which few masters could afford to do.

"But in the mode which I now propose and explain to you,

that you may fully understand it, which is the contract and agreement you are now making and taking on yourselves to perform, your master will not make you a present of an hour of your time.

"You, in reality, will have gained, and placed in his hands, previous to going out free, a sum of money, arising from your extra labor, fully sufficient to enable him to purchase an equal number of people with yourselves, man for man, woman for woman, and youth and child for youth and child, to take your place in the work of his farm, so that his work and revenue shall not be stopped or arrested for an hour, and to fit you out with all things necessary in your new life, should he think proper so to do, much to your advantage, respectability, and happiness, and to his satisfaction and honor.

"For a humane master will delight in tending to the happiness of those whom the Most High has placed under his care, and who have served him truly and faithfully.

"The only difference and change, then, which this arrangement will make in the affairs of your master, will be that he will have the same number of new servants, in the place and stead of his old and faithful ones, to do his work. You therefore now see and fully understand what my scheme for your benefit is. It is feasible and can be easily accomplished, while it will tend, at the same time, to the happiness of your lives while carrying it out and putting it into execution.

"I repeat to you again," said I to them, "that my plan is based on extra labor; that you must consider none, day or night, too great for you to perform, remembering at the same time that it is not to be accomplished in a day, but will require years of perseverance in well-doing to effect it. On my part, you may depend upon my prudence not to involve myself by speculation or otherwise, with the Divine blessing, so as to put it out of my power to carry out the agreement.

"And I will take care, by keeping regular accounts of all your gains, and by instructions to my executors, in my last will and testament, should it please God, in whose hands all things are, to take me from life before the full accomplishment of the scheme, to have our agreement truly and fully executed, and justice rendered you, by selling you out as servants for a time, and then, after the expiration of your term of service, seeing that you and your children are sent out to Liberia."

To all this, they, the whole of the adults, men and women, (no youth or child being present,) lent an attentive ear ; and again, with eyes streaming with tears, assured me of their full determination to devote their days and nights for the honor of God, the happiness of their children, and the carrying out of the plan I had devised for their benefit. It now remains for me to state the results of the experiment.

In less than six years the first half day was gained and paid for by them. In about four years, the next or second day of the week was paid for and became their own. In about two and a quarter years, the next or third day was paid for and made their own. In about fifteen months, the next day, or fourth, was theirs. In about a year, the next or fifth day was gained and paid for ; and, in about six months, the last or sixth day of the week became their own, and completed the purchase —effecting their freedom in about fourteen and a half years.

After this it took them somewhere about five months to labor, to pay the balance due on their children, added to what the youths, (boys and girls,) had earned. If there appears any discrepancy in the period in which they effected the purchase of the different days for themselves, it is to be accounted for in their drawing more money at one period than at another, as they frequently did towards the last, after they had accomplished the purchase of two or three days, or their freedom would have been sooner accomplished.

This took place, (the effecting of their freedom,) in August 1840, nearly two years since; at which time they would have taken their departure for Liberia, but as the Abolitionists of the Northern and Eastern states of our Union had occasioned much excitement in our state, not only among the owners of slaves, but among the slaves themselves, I did not consider it safe, or myself at liberty, howsoevermuch I desired it, as there was a considerable black population in the immediate neighborhood of those of my black people, to send them away.

I therefore told them, without giving them the cause, they must be satisfied to remain where they were until the proper time for their departure should arrive; with which they remained satisfied. So that they effected their freedom, as above stated, in about fourteen years and a half; and the assertion that I made in your Gazette of the 24th of June last, "that the act of sending those people away is, in my case, one of simple honesty alone," is explained in my having received in money from them, or the equivalent of money, the full price agreed on between us, for their freedom in Liberia.

Some persons, Messrs. Editors, may now, perhaps, be disposed to say, "Why proceed in this roundabout way, this giving of one-half of Saturday, this keeping of accounts, this purchasing of day after day, &c., &c.? It is all unnecessary, and their working to gain their time is all an illusion. The whole of the time of a slave belongs to his master. The master can compel his labor without freeing the slave, &c."

I admit the truth of the latter part of the assertion, that the time and labor of a slave belong to his master, but deny that the first is an illusion, as respects either the one or the other, the master or the slave; for it is founded in the moral constitution of man.

Without hope, a certain something in the future to look forward to and aspire to, man would be nothing. Deprive him of this inspiring faculty of soul, and he would grovel in the dust as a brute. But, say they, why not promise him at once freedom after fifteen years service? To this I have many and strong objections. In that mode his freedom would appear as the gift of his master, who might, as the slave would fear, repent and retract his promise.

In the other mode the slave would have gained it—have purchased and paid his master for it. Hope would be kept alive in his bosom: he would have a goal in view, continually urging him on to faithfulness, fidelity, truth, industry, economy, and every virtue and good work.

The observations of a great and good man with whom I was in correspondence, made to me in one of his letters some years since, and to whom I had faintly intimated the plan I was pursuing with my people, are so descriptive of their then situation, feelings, and conduct, that I will give you an extract from it.

"Your plan, dear sir, as I infer from what you have intimated to me, calls into action a higher and nobler motive than servile fear. It holds out a reward to the obedient and the faithful. Such a motive can seldom fail. It is the impulsive cause of all good conduct; hence we find it holding a conspicuous place in the system of government which the Almighty exercised over the ancient Israelites: 'If ye be willing and obedient, ye shall eat the good of the land.' And the same motive to Christian conduct is presented under the Christian dispensation: 'Be thou faithful unto death, and I will give thee a crown of life.'"

From the foregoing summary, it will be seen that the basis of my plan for their success and government was religion—a desire to awaken in their bosoms the love of the divinity. Hope and trust in him, once born in their souls, would produce its fruits, a determination to obedience, labor, order, economy, and all good works.

That such was the result, and was the impulsive cause of their true and faithful conduct, is shown. Its effects on the interests of their master, his happiness, is also shown and seen. They have now sailed for Liberia, the land of their fathers. I can say with truth and heartfelt satisfaction, that a more virtuous people does not exist in any community. And I pray the Most High to continue unto them the blessings which he never ceased to shower down on their heads whilst under my roof.

I will further observe, that from the day on which I made the agreement with them, notwithstanding they had, at all times previous thereto, been a well-disposed and orderly people, an entire change came over them. They were no longer apparently the same people. A sedateness, a care, an economy, an industry, took possession of them, to which there seemed to be no bounds, but in their physical strength. They were never tired of laboring, and seemed as though they could never effect enough. They became temperate, moderate, religious, setting an example of innocent and unoffending lives to the world around them, which was seen and admired by all.

The result of my experiment in a pecuniary point of view, as relates to myself, is not one of the least surprising of its features, and is this. In the space of about sixteen years which those people served me, since making the agreement with them, they have gained for me, in addition to having performed more and better labor than slaves ordinarily do in the usual time of laboring, a sum of money, including the sum they appear to have paid me in the purchase of their time, which will enable me to go to Virginia, or Carolina, and purchase a gang of people, of nearly double the number of those I have sent away.

This I state from an account kept by me, showing the amount and nature of their extra work, and labor, which I am ready to attest to, in the most solemn manner, at any time.

Previous to entering into the agreement with those people,

I calculated, and my estimate and calculation have been fully realized to me in the result, that their labor would be given with all the energy of heart, soul, and physical powers; that they would in consequence accomplish more labor in a given time than the same number of people would in ordinary circumstances; and that in addition they would labor some two, three, or four hours, morning and night, in the twenty-four of the day, more than other slaves were in the habit of doing, or would do.

To set forth and show the spirit that actuated and filled their souls in relation to their worldly concerns during the whole time they were operating under this agreement, I will state in the sequel to this some circumstances known here to hundreds of our most respectable citizens.

If the planters of Maryland, Virginia, and the Carolinas, whose lands are worn out, would entrust their slaves to the younger male branches of the family, to bring here, into our state, to cultivate the richest alluvial soils in the world, they would be enabled, under such an agreement with their slaves as I have pointed out above, after gaining by their extra labor the value of their entire gangs, to make large revenues and pass happy lives.

For I can say with great truth, that the last sixteen years of mine, passed as they have been in peace, and without anxiety, in the midst of those people, have been among the most happy of my life. The knowledge that I was surrounded by those who looked upon me in the light of a friend and father, and would willingly at any time have imperilled their own lives to save mine, if necessary, gave peace and serenity to the mind. Thus they could send their entire gangs to Liberia, without the cost of a dollar to themselves.

Besides which, to bring their slaves into this state, and keep them here, would be an act of humanity, as it would inure them to a climate very analogous to that of Africa, and they would run no risk to their health or lives when afterwards settling in Liberia.

To ensure the success of the plan in all its parts, I will say also to such masters as feel an interest in the happiness of their black people and will attempt to execute and carry it out, neglect not religious instruction to your people. Religion must be combined with the plan, and walk hand in hand with it.

I will now state, that to carry out this plan with complete success, it is all important that the slave have full and entire confidence in his master. He must be convinced that his master is his friend and well-wisher, that he is true, sincere and honest. Without this confidence of the slave in his master, the plan could not be carried out with success. It would be in vain for a master to attempt it, whose character was known for duplicity, untruth, dishonesty, or cruelty. He would not succeed in it; for no one is better acquainted with the character of his master than the slave himself.

To encourage them in the execution and carrying out of their engagement, I showed them every six months, or twice a year, their accounts, on my books, and informed them of their success, and the sum of money they had gained, which was in my hands, standing to the credit of their accounts. This proceeding on my part appeared to instill new life into them and to afford them great satisfaction. It was a proof also to them of the interest I felt in their affairs.

The Legislatures of our different slave states might, by the enactment of laws on the subject, greatly assist and protect the interest of the slave. I do not mean by forcing the master to make such arrangements or to come to such an understanding with his slaves. But in the event of misfortune or bankruptcy in the master whose slaves had been working under such an agreement, the master might be permitted to prove on his oath in a court of justice that such an agreement existed between him and his slaves, that the slaves had been working under said agreement for such and such a time, and that such a sum of money had been gained by them towards their freedom.

By which means the slaves, if seized for debt, could only be sold for a certain time, of sufficient duration, after a legal estimation, for the purpose of paying and liquidating the balance due them; well understood, that such enactments should be made by the different legislatures under the express condition that the slaves were not to remain in the United States, but to remove, or to be removed, to Liberia in Africa, as soon as the time of service for which they were sold should have expired.

If on the other hand the master of slaves, who had of his own free will entered into such an agreement with them, should die previous to the slaves having acquired the right to emigrate to Liberia, under the agreement they had made to labor for their freedom, the slaves should be protected by law, and permitted to prove in a court of justice, by one or more disinterested white persons who had heard it from the mouth of the master, the amount they had already gained under the agreement; and they should then be sold for servants for a time, to pay the balance due from them, and be forced to emigrate to Liberia.

I will now say a few words relating to my general mode of treating these people. They were lodged in warm and comfortable houses, fed with good salt provisions and corn bread, with a plenty of garden vegetables cooked with pork; clothed with strong, durable clothing, according to the season; a ration of molasses and one of salt was allowed them weekly and a little coffee and common tea every six months.

Christmas and New Year presents served to supply their

little wants, and enabled them to leave nearly everything arising from their own labor untouched in my hands. They kept hogs and fowls of their own, and cultivated what ground they needed in corn and vegetables.

In sickness, I had as good care taken of them as of myself, with good nurses to attend them. When they committed or were charged with offenses, I did not order an arbitrary punishment, but had them tried by their peers. I would summon a jury of five or six of the principal men, and say to them, "Such a man or such a woman is charged with such an offense; the witnesses, I am told, are such and such persons; summon them, hold your court, have him tried, and report to me your judgment and the punishment to be inflicted."

It was done, all in due form. The courtroom was the church. The trial took place, and the person was acquitted or condemned. The punishment awarded, if condemned and found guilty, was reported to me. I generally found it necessary to modify it, in reference to leniency. If twenty lashes were awarded, I would say to the judges, who were the executors of the sentence, "Give ten lashes and a moral lecture to the culprit for the offense."

It was done. The criminal acknowledged the justice of the punishment, promised better things for the future, and forgot not to be grateful to the master who had reduced the degree of punishment and reinstated him in place and favor.

For upwards of twenty years I have had no white man over them as an overseer. One of themselves was their manager or commander, who conducted, directed and managed the others. Nor would I myself have the time once in six months to see in person what they were doing, though the commander would report to me nightly what he had done through the day, and receive my instructions for the day following.

They were, besides, my men of business, enjoyed my confidence, were my clerks, transacted all my affairs, made purchases of materials, collected my rents, leased my houses, took care of my property and effects of every kind, and that with an honesty and fidelity that was proof against every temptation.

As I promised to state in the sequel some circumstances that would go to show the spirit that animated and filled their souls in executing and carrying out the agreement they had entered into with their master, and in what way the extra labor I have spoken of was performed, I have now to observe, that I was looked on generally by the French planters on the opposite side of the river to New Orleans, where I reside, as, if not a very cruel, at least a very severe master, one who worked his people late and early—for the whip was seldom or never heard on my plantation; never, indeed, except to uphold and support good order and morality.

Some years since, a gentleman from one of the eastern states, a friend of mine, met me in the streets of New Orleans, on a Monday, and on stopping me he began to smile, saying that he had passed the day previous, the Sabbath, in the country, a few leagues above my residence, on the right bank of the Mississippi, at the house of a rich sugar planter, who had given a party in honor of his arrival. There he had met at dinner some twenty or thirty French gentlemen, principally sugar planters on that side of the river, and their ladies.

At dinner, their conversation turned on planting, crops, slavery, etc., and he was asked what was generally thought by the inhabitants of the eastern and northern states, of the inhabitants of the south of the Union, the slave holders. The gentleman replied, among other observations, that the French planters of Louisiana were looked upon generally by the Americans of the North as very severe and even cruel masters in the treatment of their slaves, much more so even than the planters of Louisiana of English ancestry.

This brought from the gentlemen at table an assertion, that some of the most severe masters of the state were to be found among the Anglo-Americans, a term by which all Americans and strangers generally are called by the natives of Louisiana of French descent. And as an instance they cited you, mentioning your name, as one who obliged his people to work until midnight, and one or two o'clock in the morning.

For the truth of the assertion they appealed to one another, when it was confirmed by them generally, both ladies and gentlemen, who had known your black people often and often to be at work, (as they had seen them with their own eyes,) until that late hour of the night, adding, that it was known to be a common thing with them to work late and early.

The gentleman observed to the company, that the circumstance surprised and astonished him much. Knowing me as he did, he had not supposed me capable of treating my people with such severity, &c., &c. They again assured him of the fact, and appealed to every inhabitant of the country between that and my residence, for the truth.

"Now," says my friend, "I merely mention these things to you. I do not inquire as to the truth of it, because I am convinced there is some mistake about it, something I do not understand."

To this I observed, smiling, "Not so fast, my friend. All that those ladies and gentlemen said is true. They had seen, as they informed you, with their own eyes, my people at work, often and often, at the hours they mentioned to you. But did they tell you at the same time that they never saw them at work but they were as merry as crickets, singing and joyful, making the whole neighborhood vocal with their happiness?

"Had they told you that, which would have been nothing but the truth, it would no doubt have convinced you that there was no compulsion in their laboring. The only part of the assertion of these ladies and gentlemen which was incorrect, was that I obliged my slaves to work until midnight and until one and two in the morning. They are often working, I confess, at these hours, but I do not force them to work, it is of their own free will and accord."

"Then," observed the gentleman, "you must pay them, I presume." "I do not say," said I to him, "what I do, further than that there is no compulsion in their laboring. But I promise that you shall know the story one day, if I am spared,"— which he will, as I shall send him a copy of this.

We then separated, but I found the gentleman, I confess, very incredulous, notwithstanding that he knew something of my character, as to slaves working of their own accord, without compulsion from their masters. The story is this.

My residence is on the opposite side of the river Mississippi, immediately in front of the centre of the city of New Orleans. The steam ferry which runs from one side of the river to the other lands a short distance below my house. The French ladies and gentlemen, residing above my house, on the right bank of the river, being very fond of balls and theatres, were in consequence in the constant habit of passing and repassing my house, to and from the city of New Orleans, in their carriages, at all hours of the night and morning.

Immediately below and adjoining my residence, I had extensive establishments for the making of brick, engaged in working in which, those ladies saw, with their own eyes, often and often, my people, at the hours they mentioned; which explains why they considered me a severe master.

I have to observe that I was in the habit of never retiring to rest at night until seeing my commander, and knowing that the people had come in from their work; for I have labored myself, night and day, through a long life, and shall continue to do so to its close. And often and often, when the clock would strike ten and eleven, I would say to a servant of the house, not having seen the commander, "Have the people come in from their work?"

"No, sir," he would reply, "I see bonfires in the brickyard. They have not yet finished their work." I would say to him, "Go out and ask the commander what keeps him out so late." He would return to me, saying, "Sir, the commander says there are some thirty or forty thousand bricks out, the weather looks like rain, and he must get them in and save them, or they will all be lost."

Satisfied with this statement I have waited till midnight and sent out again. The same answer returned; again at one o'clock in the morning, the same answer; they singing the whole time, that they might be heard over the neighborhood.

At two o'clock I have sent out to him with positive orders to break off work and bring his people in, even if the bricks should be lost—that I would not permit them to work any longer. When in would come the commander, and likely not at all pleased, saying, "Sir, if you had allowed us to go on an hour or two longer we should have saved all our brick, which I fear we may lose." This will serve to show how the spirit worked within them. After retiring to bed and rest, I have known them hundreds of times, on appearance of rain, arise and go out to work, at all hours of the night and morning.

I will now give another instance, (I might relate hundreds,) going to show the effect of that hope, that charm of man's existence, liberty, on the life and actions of those people.

Some years since some twenty or thirty of those people were engaged in erecting some extensive brick warehouses on Julia street in New Orleans, (for they were excellent mechanics of various trades, and were in the habit of making brick, purchasing shells and burning lime, sawing timber, and then taking the materials when made, and building them up into fine houses on both sides of the river, for their master,) near to the residence of Edward E. Parker, Esq., one of our most wealthy and respectable citizens, a gentleman who was in the habit of building very extensively himself in the city.

Meeting Mr. Parker on a certain day in the street of New Orleans I was accosted and asked, whether I would sell him a certain black man named Jim, or James. Having several men of that name I inquired which James, when he observed, the one that was at the head of the bricklayers who were erecting those warehouses on Julia street, near his residence.

I replied to him, no, that I was not in the habit of selling people, that I purchased occasionally but never sold. Mr. Parker then observed that he wished I would depart in the present instance from my general rule and agree to sell him that man; that he was very desirous of possessing him; that as he was erecting several buildings the man would suit him and he would give a good price for him.

I again said to him that the man was not for sale, and was about to leave him when he observed: "Could you not be tempted to sell him, sir? I will give you two thousand five hundred dollars for him in cash." I told Mr. Parker it did not tempt me, and we separated.

A week or two thereafter I met Mr. Parker again, and was again accosted on the same subject, with, "Do, Mr. McDonogh, sell me that man. I will give you three thousand dollars for him."

Again I made him him the same answer, that he was not for sale. Again and again we met in the streets, and each time the same request, raising the offer of price at each interview, until at last Mr. Parker informed me that he would pay me five thousand dollars in cash for him. Feeling at length a little vexed at these repeated demands, I said to Mr. Parker, "Though you are a very rich man, sir, your whole fortune could not purchase that man, or any of the others. He is not to be sold."

Mr. Parker finding at length, from the refusal of such a large sum of money for him, that there was no hope of obtaining him, observed to me, "Well then Mr. McDonogh, seeing that you will not sell him at any price, tell me what kind of people are those of yours." To which I replied, "How so, Mr. Parker? I suppose they are like other men, flesh and blood, like you and myself."

He replied, "Why, sir, I have never seen such people. Building, as they are, next door to my residence, I see and have my eyes on them from morning till night. You are never there, for I have never met you or seen you once at the building. Tell me, sir, where do those people of yours live? Do they cross the river morning and night?"

I informed him that they lived on the opposite side of the river, where I lived myself, and crossed it to their work, when working in New Orleans, night and morning, except when stormy, (which happened very seldom,) when I did not permit them to cross it and endanger their lives; at such times they remained at home or in the city.

"Why, sir," said he, "I am an early riser, getting up before day. And do you think that I am not awakened every morning of my life by the noise of their trowels, at work, and their singing and noise, long before day? And do you suppose, sir, that they stop or leave off work at sundown? No, sir. They work as long as they can see to lay brick and then carry up brick and mortar for an hour or two afterwards to be ahead of their work the next morning.

"And again, sir, do you think that they walk at their work? No, sir, they run all day. You see, sir, those immensely long ladders five stories in height? Do you suppose they walk up them? No, sir, they run up and down like monkeys the whole day long. I never saw such people as those, sir. I do not know what to make of them.

"Was there a white man over them with a whip in his hands all day, why then I should see and understand the cause of their running and incessant labor. But I cannot comprehend it, sir. There is something in it, sir, there is something in it. Great man, sir, that Jim—great man, sir,—should like to own him, sir, should like to own him."

After having laughed very heartily at the observations of Mr. Parker, for it was all truth, every word of it, I informed him that there was a secret about it, which I would disclose to him some day; and we separated. Now, Mr. Parker imputed the conduct of these people, (for I have given the very words and expressions he used, and he is alive, hearty and well, in New Orleans, and can be spoken to by any one interested in the subject,) to the head man who conducted them, and in consequence, impressed with this belief, offered me five thousand dollars for him.

But Mr. Parker knew not the stimulus that acted on the heart of each and every one of them; that it was the whole body of them that moved together as one mind, not alone the head man, as he supposed.

In closing this statement I will say a few words to show what the attachment of people similarly situated will be to a master who treats them justly. The ship on which they sailed for Africa lay opposite my house, in the Mississippi, at the bank of the river. I had taken my leave of them when they went on board the ship on Friday evening, the day previous to her sailing, in my house.

The scene which then took place I will not attempt to describe—it can never be erased from memory. Though standing in need on the occasion of consolation myself, in bidding a last farewell on earth to those who had so many claims on my affections, and who had been around and about me for such a long series of years, I had to administer it to them, who stood in the greater need of it.

I had to tell them that the separation was but for a brief period of time; that we should meet again, I trusted, in a better and happier state; to charge them to gird up their loins and play the man valiantly, in their determination to enter their own Canaan; and to remember that there was still another and final separation from all things earthly, which they had to sustain and encounter, to meet and be prepared for which they should persevere in well-doing to the end; that their lamps must be kept well trimmed, and their lights burning.

On Saturday morning, the Rev. Mr. McLain, the Agent of the American Colonization Society, who took deep interest in all that concerned this people, crossed the river to dispatch the ship, and see them take their departure, which took place about eight o'clock in the morning of that day, the 11th of June. After seeing them off, the ship was taken by a steamer.

Mr. McLain came into my house, as I was expecting him to breakfast. On seeing him much affected, tears standing in his eyes, I inquired if anything had taken place to give him pain; to which he replied:

"Oh, sir, it was an affecting sight to see them depart. They were all on the deck of the ship, and your servants who have not gone were on the shore bidding them farewell. From every tongue on board the ship I heard the charge to those on shore, 'Fanny, take care of our master; James, take care of our master, take care of our master; as you love us, and hope to meet us in heaven, take care of our beloved master.'"

Which ejaculations, said he, continued until they were out of sight. This would appear to reverse the general course of things. It is the master or mistress who is heard, when about to take a voyage, recommending their servants to the care of some confidential person.   But here were the servants recommending their master to the care of other servants.

I have now, Messrs. Editors, fulfilled my promise, and related the experience I have had in the management of slaves. Should it induce but one planter in the state to try the mode I pursued so much to my own satisfaction and pecuniary advantage, and meet with the same success which has attended my attempt, I shall consider the time it has cost in giving the relation well spent, and myself fully repaid.

With great respect, I am, gentlemen,
Your friend and obedient servant,
JOHN McDONOGH.

FROM MRS. SARAH BELLA McLEAN.

(WIFE OF JOHN M'LEAN, JUSTICE OF THE SUPREME COURT.)

Washington City, February 10, 1844.

Mr. John McDonogh :—

I need not apologize for addressing you, my dear friend. I feel convinced that my correspondence is acceptable to you, and I know that you have thought of me frequently, wondering perhaps at my silence. I assure you, that you are very often present in my mind. I cannot forget your philanthropy, your extraordinary and most praiseworthy exertions in behalf of the slaves, your kind, considerate heart, and your benevolent intentions. May God abundantly reward you for both in time and in eternity!

I cannot yet cease to regret that I had not the pleasure of seeing you when in New Orleans. Such an opportunity may never again be afforded to me. I have much to say which I find difficult to write. Your suggestion respecting a female colonization society I mentioned to several ladies of Cincinnati, and it was heard with great approbation and commended as an excellent missionary work. Africa is in darkness and no doubt is destined in the providence of God to feel the light of truth and civilization.

But with us funds are difficult to procure, and transportation is expensive. We cannot of course influence the slave, and the free colored families are unwilling to go to Africa, and we have no power to force them. In consideration of all these difficulties there was a society formed for the purpose of improving the black population of the state of Ohio. We keep an agent employed whose business it is to visit every black settlement and town and farm for the purpose of instructing them more perfectly in agriculture, the mechanic arts, and morals and religion.

They also establish schools and provide teachers for them. They organize Sunday schools and instruct them generally in regard to all duties civil and social. The tendency of this is to benefit the white as well as the black population. I think in the state of Ohio there are upwards of 17,000 colored persons. Of course, were they left in ignorance and vice they would be a dangerous kind of citizens, infinitely more so than when under a system of instruction and moral improvement.

In this way, my friend, are we not preparing missionaries, perhaps for Africa? Are we not in the performance of duty? Yes, I think I hear you say, we are. I would with pleasure advance the Colonization Society. I am member of one, and I have the highest respect for its object and its members, but it appears more properly to belong to the slave states, as in the free states we can use no compulsion.

I make this very long explanation to convince you that I have not been regardless of your very excellent advice, and also at the same time to call your attention to the importance of educating the emigrants preparatory to their leaving for Africa. There is an admirable school and college in the north grant of the state of Ohio, where persons of color, male and female, can be received and educated at a moderate expense and fitted for usefulness. And what better benevolence could be devised, my friend, than to send twenty or thirty or more young persons of this unfortunate portion of God's creatures to be thus improved and fitted for extensive usefulness?

I feel convinced that your generous heart will at once see the blessing this would yield both to you and to them. Do not, my friend, leave all the good deeds of this kind to be performed by your executors. Pardon me in urging you to do as much as you can while you are living, and enjoy the sweet pleasure it will afford. You might endow a college for the exclusive education of colored children and locate it in Ohio. I shall be happy to assist you in every way in my power.

Let me know if you are willing to make some such appropriation and I will assist you in devising a plan. One idea is to send pupils to Oberlin; another, to assist our society for the promotion of useful knowledge among the black population of Ohio. It is called the Ohio Ladies' Society for the Education of Colored Persons, of which I am the president.

I know you will pardon all this, my friend. I am influenced to make these representations to you from the love of God and the admiration of your kind heart and generous intentions. Will you oblige me by answering this very soon? And believe me your very sincere friend and well wisher,

SARAH BELLA MCLEAN.

P. S. Present my compliments and best respects to Mr. Bennett. You of course recognize in my new name the former

MRS. GARNARD.

FROM MRS. McLEAN.

Washington City, March 14, 1844.

Mr. John McDonogh,
    Dear Friend :—

I wrote you several weeks ago. From your long silence I fear the letter has miscarried or, which would be infinitely more painful to me, you may have been dissatisfied with its contents. I can scarcely imagine how this could arise, feeling all that I said was dictated by the most profound respect for your mind and heart, and at the same time written with the spirit of kindness and Christian charity.

Indeed it was simply a reply to the suggestions and inquiries contained in your last letter. I beg you will be convinced of my deep interest for your happiness, and the happiness and prosperity of all the servants and dependents by whom you are surrounded and to whose welfare you are devoting time and thought. I fervently pray that the Almighty may abundantly bless you with his protecting care, and that he may strengthen your benevolent resolves and actions, which produce in your mind that peace of conscience which is far above all treasures.

My dear friend, will you pardon me in the hope that you are making preparation for that spiritual world to which we are approaching. Do not delay it. There is nothing in our possession so uncertain as time. Can you not visit the western country this summer? It will give us great pleasure to see you in Cincinnati. I will treat you with the kindness of a sister and my family will do all in their power to minister to your comfort.

Allow me, my friend, to insist upon this. I wish to see you and talk over your plans of benevolence in the disposition of the great estate which God in his mercy has enabled you to accumulate. How much you have in your possession with which to bless the poor injured Africans! I fervently thank heaven that it is in your heart to undertake the great work. Your next letter, I hope, will inform me of your health and the engagements that are at present occupying your attention.

I shall be glad to receive any advice from you on the subject of colonization, or anything that you may advance on other subjects in the cause of philanthropy. Present my respects to your valuable friend Mr. Bennett. We leave Washington City in a few days for Cincinnati. Judge McLean sends his kind regards to you. And now, farewell. I remain your sincere friend,

With sentiments of the highest esteem,
SARAH BELLA McLEAN.

TO MRS. McLEAN.

New Orleans, May 6, 1844.

Mrs. Sarah Bella McLean,
Madam :—

Receive I pray you a thousand thanks for the very kind and friendly letters of the 10th of February and 14th of March last which you have done me the honor to address me, and be assured that I prize and appreciate them, coming as they do from one so amiable and highly gifted.

Permit me at the same time, madam, though late, to offer you congratulations, and through you to Judge McLean, on your happy union. I heard of it through the public prints at the time it took place, and greatly rejoiced at your happiness. That it will tend to the honor of our adorable Master, I feel and know; for the marriage of his children is decreed and their union predestinated in heaven. All such then as are joined in love here below by the Holy Spirit are blessed, made agents of doing good here on earth, and must be happy.

I have to apologize to you, madam, in not having replied at a more early date to your interesting and most friendly letters. The cause was, in the first place, you informed me that you expected to leave Washington for Cincinnati on or about the 15th of March, and I feared my letter if I had written would not have found you there. Secondly, a prolonged absence from the city into the country has put it out of my power.

And thirdly, forced as I am during daylight to attend to a mass of business affairs almost beyond my physical powers to sustain at my advanced period of life, and which admits of no delay, I am in consequence obliged to do all my writing at night, with eyes fast failing me. I am writing these few lines to you, madam, at midnight. I am therefore assured, madam, amiable and forgiving as you are, of your pardon and forgiveness in advance.

The society which I took the liberty of recommending to you, madam, to establish in Cincinnati is not a branch society to the ladies' society for the purpose of educating the children of the colonists and natives of Liberia in Africa by sending out free colored teachers to open schools there. The society you mentioned to me, madam, as having been formed for the improvement of the free colored population of Ohio in all that concerns their religious, civil and social state, merits high commendation, and with the blessing of the Most High must be the means of great good to them as well as to the whites.

I am greatly charmed, madam, to hear you say, (for no one has it more in their power from your talent and your heart to do it service than you have,) speaking of the African Colonization Society, that you are its warm friend, are a member of one, and would by all means in your power advance its cause. It is indeed a holy cause, and has the smile of Heaven upon it.

You inform me that there is an admirable school and college in the north part of your state where persons of color can be received, educated, and fitted for usefulness, and recommend me to send some young persons to that institution, and not to leave all the good deeds of the kind to be performed by my executors. You further observe that I might endow a college exclusively for colored children in Ohio, and propose to me a choice of four plans of usefulness, any or all of which I might patronize and carry out.

The extent of your philanthropy and the goodness of your heart, madam, I acknowledge shine forth in every word you have uttered, but a very humble individual like myself, with limited means at command whatever my desires might be, cannot do and accomplish all things. Time and numbers accomplish what few individuals have it in their power to do. Africa I confess to you madam, is one of my favorite daughters. But, strong as are her claims, she is not my chief favorite, for charity begins at home.

Though I refuse not my little mite, as I wend my way along the path of life, to the unhappy and unfortunate whom I overtake in the road, still the chief object I aim at is to husband, amass and take care of the goods which the Most High gives me, not placing my affection on them I trust, but husbanding them until the day of my departure arrives. Events indeed may turn up, for all that poor-sighted mortal can see, which may determine me to disclose it sooner.

You will then know, madam, for what object the very humble individual whom you have honored with the appellation of friend has lived; and, I hope, not to condemn, but to approbate and approve.

Whilst on the subject of your recommendation, education, I will observe that under the laws of our state owners of slaves not being permitted to educate them, I applied some ten or twelve years since by memorial to the legislature for permission to educate them under the obligation of bond and security to send all such to Africa within five years from the date of the law. But I was refused the permission.

Finding that, I determined to secure to them and their descendants education by other means, and in consequence sent two talented young men of seventeen and eighteen years of age (slaves and black as Africa) to the college of Lafayette, at Easton in Pennsylvania. The president of this institution was the excellent and talented Doctor Junkin, whom you probably are acquainted with, as he now resides in your state, being the president of the University at Oxford, not far from your city.

One of those young men, (both of whom are destined for the ministry,) his education being completed, has departed for Africa, and is now at the mission station at Settra Kroo, Liberia, keeping a school for the native youth. I frequently hear from him, and his letters are most interesting and satisfying.

The other young man is still at Easton college, where it is expected he will graduate the ensuing September or October. In addition to his college studies, for he possesses talent of a high order, he is studying medicine and surgery under Doctor Abernethy, and will become, I trust, a celebrated physician, divine, and teacher of the classics and several of the modern languages, in all of which he is nearly perfect.

In a late letter from the Honorable Walter Lowrie, of New York, to whose care I had sent these two young men, he gives me an extract from a letter he had just received from David, the name of the young man who is yet at the Lafayette College. As it shadows out in strong relief the mind of this young African, I copy it for your perusal. Mr. Lowrie says:

"David is himself fully alive to the prospects before him. In his letter before me he writes: 'When I have obtained those two professions, that is, theological and medical, I will go with a glad and overflowing heart to that once enlightened but now benighted land, with the Holy Bible in one hand and my box of medicine in the other. With the one, I will strive to cure their souls, preaching from its inspired pages the everlasting gospel of good tidings of great joy which shall be to all people, peace on earth and good will towards men; and with the other, their bodies, striving to heal their wounds and bruises, and to dispel their fevers and other diseases.' These, sir, are noble resolves. God in his infinite mercy grant they may be fully carried out and realized in his life."

I have the pleasure to inform you, madam, of the arrival of a ship here from Liberia, commanded by Capt. Hamburg, a very gentlemanly man, bringing me letters highly pleasing from that part of my black family which I had sent there. He informs me that he has seen them all, and had dined frequently with them at their houses. They informed him that they were happy, and were in possession of everything they could desire, fine plantations, etc.

When they were inquired of by him if they were desirous of returning to Louisiana, their reply was, that they would willingly cross the sea again to see once more their master before they died, but for all things else they would not change Africa for any country on earth.

Now, madam, in view of those declarations and this happiness, for this part of my family, now there, were happy when here, permit me to ask you why the abolitionists oppose the Colonization Society, the colonization scheme, and why they oppose a removal of the colored people of our country to Africa, that great country, the land of their fathers, where they may indeed be happy.

Do, madam, in the name of Africa, I beseech you, as well as in the name of our country, for their removal concerns the two races of men, exert your potent influence with the abolitionists of your great state, to induce them to advocate the removal of the free colored man and to assist him to Africa, where alone he can live in peace, and in the enjoyment of freedom and happiness; for he never can live in peace or safety with the white man on the same soil as a free man.

In your last letter you observe that, not having heard from me in reply to your first, you fear that letter must have miscarried, or that I have been dissatisfied with its contents. Neither, madam, took place. I both received it and was charmed with its contents, acknowledging as I do with gratitude the honor you did me in every line. The invitation you have given me, madam, to visit Cincinnati, and the expressions of kindness and regard with which you were pleased to accompany it, demand my warmest acknowledgments, and lay me under obligations which I shall never be able to repay.

I would, madam, that my hand could trace on paper the feelings of my heart. But it cannot. All it can do is to repeat again my thanks, and say, should it ever be my good fortune to reach within a hundred miles of your residence it should be traversed to make you my respects and offer to you the thanks and gratitude of an overflowing heart.

Your kind expressions, madam, bring to my recollection some dearly beloved sisters, to whom for twenty years previous to 1830 I yearly promised, with a full determination to perform, that the ensuing spring I would see them. But that spring has never yet set in. Each successive one from that to this, found me deeper and deeper immersed in the affairs of life ; and those beloved sisters, living in my native city of Baltimore, I have not seen for forty-four years. In 1830 I gave up all hope of ever seeing them in this life, and so wrote them.

Still, I hope to sleep there, for my ambition reaches no further now than the desire of lying down alongside those (that my ashes may mix with theirs) beloved parents, my father and mother, who sleep there and were more to me during life than all things else on earth. Pardon me, madam, if I have digressed so far from the subject of your interesting letters. The recollections were awakened in my mind by the endearing term sister which you have had the kindness to trace in characters which breathed through the epistles.

Present my best respects, I pray you, madam, to Judge McLean, and say that I reciprocate in the warmest manner all the kind wishes he has had the goodness to express towards me. And with sentiments of high and profound respect, and every wish for your happiness, I have the honor to be, madam,
Your most devoted servant and friend,
JOHN McDONOGH.

TO MRS. McLEAN.

New Orleans, October 21, 1844.
Mrs. Sarah Bella McLean,

Madam :—Permitted by your indulgent goodness the honor of your correspondence, I was about to forward you a few slips out of our public prints here, going to show the happiness and prosperity of the inhabitants of Liberia, Africa, (and which you will please find enclosed,) when the great pleasure I enjoyed in addressing you a long letter on the 6th of May last, in reply to your several interesting letters, was brought to my recollection.

At the same time my fears awoke that it had miscarried and had never reached you, or still more unfortunate indeed that I might have said something in it in an unguarded moment that might have displeased you, which, if so, would be to me a source of deep regret and mortification.

I have now the pleasure to say to you, madam, that since last addressing you I have received by the brig Lime Rock, arrived here about the middle of August from Monrovia, Liberia, a number of letters from the black people whom I sent there expressing the highest satisfaction at their situation and prospects.

A suit at law which interests the poor, and which of a consequence will interest you, madam, for your heart is the seat of feeling, charity and benovolence, will be tried early in the session of the Supreme Court here. It is a just, holy cause, and involves a large property which is intended by me, as I have said, for the poor. As you will be shortly in Washington, (I cannot but regret that ladies do not practise law, as I should most assuredly, were that the case, madam, apply for your assistance in the defence of a cause which interests the unfortunate,) permit me then, madam, to pray a line from you in relation to it after your arrival in that city.

General Jones and Mr. Meredith are charged to carry it on for me. A word from you, madam, to either of those gentlemen, should you meet them in society, would secure their zealous exertions in that cause and be forever remembered by me. Be pleased, madam, to present my respects to Judge McLean, and believe me to be with profound respect,

Your most devoted servant and friend,

JOHN McDONOGH.

TO MRS. McLEAN.

New Orleans, February 20, 1846.

Mrs. Sarah Bella McLean,

Madam :— I have the honor to acknowledge the receipt of your greatly esteemed favors of the 23rd August and 1st January last, which afforded me, as everything which comes from your pen and heart does, the highest gratification, and more especially, as they informed me at the same time of your health being entirely restored and that Judge McLean was in full enjoyment of his.

I have again to apologize to you, madam, for having failed to acknowledge for such a length of time the receipt of your most kind, friendly, and interesting letters, but am assured in advance, good and amiable as you are, of your forgiveness, when informed of the causes which led to it. Within the last few months I have had much to affect me, much to show that life here below is a shadow, that all things are fleeting and vain but virtue and the love of the Deity.

But why should I give pain to you, or interrupt for a moment the happiness of one who honors me with her correspondence, feeling as I do that all I can write must be of a sombre character, tinged with the melancholy that affects and weighs down my spirits! Still I will proceed, for you honor me also with your friendship and kind regards, and it will give ease to my heart, selfish as I am, to unburthen its regrets and laments unto you.

I have been blessed through life with spirits of great elasticity, and strove to receive the dispensations of the Most High, whatever they might be, with a heart humble and resigned to his will. But I know not how it is or whence was the cause; loss of health perhaps, for I have been lately much unwell, or advance of old age and consequent feebleness of mind and body. I find that my equanimity and vigor of mind, though I trust my heart is entirely resigned to the divine will, is now more easily disturbed and shaken than it formerly was.

Amongst many circumstances of an unpleasant and afflicting nature which have occurred lately to disturb the even tenor of my way to the land of delight and peace, has been the departure of one of those beloved sisters, of whom I spoke to you in one of my former letters, to the world of spirits. It was only a month or two before her departure that she saw cut down in the springtime of life a beloved son and daughter, the son in the twenty-fifth year of his age, the daughter in the twenty-third, leaving behind her a husband and three children to lament their early loss.

On hearing of her affliction under this dispensation I wrote her a few lines, sympathizing with her, and telling her that her children had only preceded her a few short days. Little indeed did I expect that the next account would inform me of her departure. As she was greatly beloved by me, and worthy of all love for the greatness of her virtues, for she was my companion, my friend in childhood and youth, with whom I walked hand in hand and took sweet counsel, I will enclose you a copy of my last letter to her.

Excuse all this, madam. It eases my heart to speak of one pure and lovely spirit, who possessed the love of my heart at a period of life when the affections are all warm, innocent and pure, to another pure and lovely spirit, her counterpart in the virtues of truth, faith, charity and love. I feel, however, that I have done wrong in having addressed you as I have done. If my letters can not be written so as to conduce to your satisfaction, I at least should be on my guard not to overcast your brow with a cloud or occasion you one moment of pain or unhappiness.

You observe, not having heard from me in reply to your last letter, that you fear you may have offended me in some of the recommendations made therein. That, madam, is impossible. Nothing that you could say could give offense. Your suggestions and recommendations, proofs of the wisdom and the goodness of your heart, have at all times, on the contrary, afforded me the greatest pleasure, and tended to augment in a high degree the admiration which I have always entertained of the loveliness of your character. I have always considered myself most fortunate and highly honored in your friendly counsel and advice.

If I prove an irregular correspondent—and I acknowledge my sin, pleading in extenuation age and a mass of business affairs almost beyond my strength—do not I pray you, madam, let that deprive me of the pleasure of being often in the receipt of your highly prized and interesting letters.

A thousand thanks for your friendly invitation to make you a visit. Nothing, I pray you to be assured, madam, would afford me more pleasure. But I fear I shall not be able to realize it in this world. We shall meet, though, I feel assured, madam, in another land, a better one. Occupied here below, as our souls I trust are, for the promotion of the honor and glory of our blessed Lord and Master, by striving to bring the souls of men to him, our spirits will meet, I trust, and recognize each other, in the realms above, as fellow laborers in this glorious cause.

For myself, if I have desired life, it has been that I might tend to the honor and glory of him who made and placed me here. And if, after he retires me from this scene, it shall be found on a review of my actions that I have not lived in vain, then will the object of my soul through its whole existence here have been accomplished.

Many thanks, madam, for the kind regards of Judge

McLean. I note your observations in relation to Judge McLean, and the black people of the late John Randolph of Virginia, with your recommendations to him, for which I thank you. All you do or say, madam, is in wisdom. A sojournment in Ohio for a few years by those people that they may acquire a knowledge of God, join the church of Christ our Lord, receive the education of our schools, and acquire a knowledge of husbandry and the arts of life, would most assuredly be nearly everything for them.

But, madam, there is something further requisite to secure the happiness of that unfortunate race here in life, and that of their posterity—to secure indeed their future safety and existence on earth. Looking at the present state of these people among us, in the free as well as the slave states of the Union, is not enough. We should reflect on what their state will be in fifty or one hundred years to come. You, madam, who can do so much, by your wisdom and influence in your great state, for this people, have you reflected on their situation and what is to become of them in times to come?

My own opinion is, I have long entertained it, and every day's observations confirm it more strongly on my mind, that without separation of the races, extermination of one or the other must inevitably take place. The two races can never inhabit together in a state of equality the same country. They may for a short time, even in the capacity of master and slave; as equals and brethren, never.

Then, madam, is it not the province of wisdom to remove and separate them in time, and that more especially when they have a country of their own to go to, one of the finest quarters of the earth, where they may be happy and they and their families live in safety? Could not the Congress of the United States be induced to do something for them, and that without interfering with the rights of property? Could it not pass laws for the benefit of the black man? Indeed both races, white and black, are equally interested in the separation.

I have sometimes thought that that body might be induced to pass a law something similar to this, say appropriating out of our immense store of land a million of acres, (in the first instance, as a trial, to see how the plan would work,) which might be sold at government price; and slave owners invited to bring in their slaves, say to an office in the city of Washington, and deliver them up to the government and receive a certain price for them (according to a tariff fixed by law, classing them males, females and children of different ages at different prices) payable in scrip, said scrip payable at once in land out of the million of acres so appropriated, or otherwise in money as the land is sold and money received for it.

The views that I take on the subject are that the law should establish very low prices to be paid for the slaves, and merely invite such slaveholders as thought proper to take in their slaves and deliver them up to the government. As the government now keeps a fleet on the coast of Africa, and has ships constantly sailing from the ports of the United States to that coast, it would cost very little to transport them there and deliver them up to the African colonization societies in Liberia.

My opinion is, great numbers of the slave holders would take in their black people and deliver them up to the government, though they might receive but a very small price in payment for them.

This opinion is founded on the knowledge that great numbers of the slave holders would even now deliver up their slaves to the American Colonization Society to go to Africa without receiving any indemnity for them, if their circumstances admitted it. But being somewhat in debt they cannot, as honest men, do so; but could they receive even a very low price, it would enable them to pay their debts and benefit their people at the same time, which certainly great numbers, with thanks given to God, would seize the opportunity of doing.

I have thrown these undigested ideas together, madam, which I am afraid you will scarcely understand, and will beg the favor of you, if you approve of them, to mention them to Judge McLean, seeing that by his great and deserved influence he has it in his power to serve this unfortunate race. If the senators and representatives in Congress from your state, a non-slaveholding state, would bring forward such a law, I should think there would be no difficulty in passing it.

As to an appropriation of a million of acres of land, the government having so much of it, it would be as nothing. Besides where could such a noble use, in the sight of both God and man, be found for the store? or who of the race of man can say that great store has not been given to us, in the secret and all wise purposes of the Most High, to be applied to this express purpose?

It is about four months since I last heard from my friends in Liberia. They were then all well, were happy, had increased considerably in numbers, and express fervent thanks, love, and gratitude to the great Giver of all good for his continued and wonderful blessings to them.

Now, madam, I again pray you to favor me often with your letters. Write me in the same frank and friendly manner you have hithertofore done. Give me your views, counsel, and advice on everything which interests the great subject which should be the grand object of our existence on earth, that of tending in the highest possible degree to the honor and glory of our adorable Lord and Master, in bringing souls to him and doing good on earth. Fear not giving offense. That is impossible.

For all your kind wishes and regards, (for the prayers of the good and virtuous are heard at the Throne of Grace,) accept, I pray, my warmest thanks, and be assured they are fervently reciprocated with you. Present my best respects, I pray you, madam, to Judge McLean. Say to him that his name is heard in the south on the lips of the good, virtuous, and influential, when speaking of the Presidency, as one who if placed there—and they hope to see him at the next vacancy filling the chair of Washington—would tend to the honor, prosperity, and happiness of his country, and that none would hear of his being a candidate for that high appointment with greater satisfaction and joy than myself.

With profound respect, I am, madam, your obliged and devoted servant,

J. McDONOGH.

FROM REV. ROBERT S. FINLEY.

New Orleans, Saturday, April 9, 1847.

My dear Sir:—

Bishop Hawks of St. Louis and other influential gentlemen have expressed a desire that I should republish in the Liberian Advocate your letter giving an account of the management of those servants you sent to Liberia. I have determined to do so, as I believe that document produced a more profound impression in favor of the African colonization than any paper that has appeared for many years.

But I should like to publish it with another letter from you giving an account of the condition and prospects of your servants since their arrival in Liberia. The present circulation of my paper, the Liberian Advocate, is five thousand, but if you would consent to write me such a letter as above indicated, to accompany your first letter, I would publish an edition of ten thousand copies, if I could raise the means of paying the expense of the extra copies.

I expect to be in New Orleans about two weeks, and to hold a series of meetings in behalf of the Colonization Society. I expect to deliver a discourse to-morrow afternoon in the Methodist Episcopal Church at four o'clock p. m. A public meeting of the Louisiana Colonization Society will also be held on Tuesday night for the election of officers. At this meeting we expect addresses from distinguished citizens. Could you not favor the meeting with your presence?

I am very desirous to see you and obtain your views on several important subjects connected with colonization in Africa, especially in reference to its commercial importance. When and where would it be agreeable for you to meet me? A letter addressed to me to the care of "Henderson & Peale" would reach me with dispatch.

Very respectfully your friend,
ROBERT S. FINLEY.

TO REV. ROBERT S. FINLEY.

New Orleans, June 9, 1847.

Dear Sir:—

As you requested, I have written the letter herein enclosed, marked No. 1, giving you the information you desire, and which is intended for publication, if you approve of it, with my letter on African colonization.

You will also receive herewith eleven other letters, from the people I have helped to reach their fatherland, which, with the four letters I handed you in person, make fifteen, for publication. One of those letters I have just received by the return of the Mary Wilks, which took out the last emigrants from this to Liberia. By this letter you will perceive that the writer, George Ellis, sends me a little coffee, the product of his own trees, and those trees raised from the seed planted by himself since his arrival in Africa, now five years, and which now yield, as he informs me, a half a pound to a pound each tree. The coffee is of delicious quality. I hand our mutual friend a little of it to forward you.

In looking over those letters I found in one of them a copy of a letter written by me to Washington in reply to his letters of the 1st and 29th of November, 1844, and March 12, 1845, which I have enclosed for your perusal, if you can decipher it, as it will tend to show the spirit which actuates and has actuated me towards those people. If you think good will arise from its publication, you are at liberty to publish it with their letters; if you think otherwise, suppress it.

When last I had the pleasure of conversing with you, I promised to give you an extract from a letter of mine written to a lady some time since throwing out some points in relation to a mode by which the Congress of the United States might act on the subject of colonization, which in my opinion would be approved of by every section of our country, north and south, slave holder and non-slaveholder, and men of every creed.

This I will strive to do shortly, as I desire to send the enclosed to you without further delay. My time being so taken up by business, it is seldom I can devote a moment to this.

       With great respect, I am, dear sir,
         Your friend and obedient servant,
                  JOHN McDONOGH.
The Rev. Robert S. Finley, D. D.,
    Saint Louis, Mo.

TO REV. ROBERT S. FINLEY.

New Orleans, June 9, 1847.

Dear Sir :—

I have the pleasure to acknowledge the receipt of your esteemed favor of the 9th of April last, informing me of your intention to publish another edition of my letters on African colonization, and saying that you are very desirous of publishing at the same time with it an account of the present conditions, state of happiness and prospects of the servants I sent to Liberia, if I would favor you with a letter on the subject.

To this I will observe, sir, that it will afford me great pleasure in complying with your request, as far as in my power. The information I possess on that subject is to me of the most pleasing and satisfactory nature. It is derived from a correspondence with themselves, receiving letters, as I do, by every vessel that arrives from that part of the African coast where they are settled, and from conversations with various gentlemen who have lately been trading there, who have seen them, been on their plantations and in their houses, who had known some of them previous to their departure from this country, and were the bearers of messages and letters from them to me.

In those letters written by themselves, for many of them write and write well, some of them having become my clerks here, they state, as do the gentlemen who have seen them, that they are contented and happy, have plantations under cultivation, with good houses, various kinds of domestic animals, every necessary of life (with the exception of clothing, which is scarce and dear in that country) in the greatest abundance, and scarcely anything to desire or wish for.

They enjoy good health, having had but little sickness since their arrival in Africa. The climate is a good one for the black man, and the soil one of great fertility and richness. Fruitful as is the valley of the Mississippi, and North America in general, still it is not to compare in fruitfulness to that part of Africa, as their soil yields them two or three crops a year. They give me in their letters long lists of vegetables which include nearly every article raised in the United States, besides vast numbers of tropical products which our climate does not produce.

In short, they say that Africa is one of the finest quarters of the world, and nothing could induce them to remove from it for a residence in any other country. Their letters also state, for there are several men of observation among them, that their country is destined in a few years to carry on and support a very considerable commerce; that the attention of the colonists is now turned to the opening of roads and rivers into the interior, by which routes the products of the forest and soil will be brought to the seaboard and exchanged for the manufactures of Europe and America.

Since writing the foregoing, sir, it strikes me, on reflection, that the publishing of the original letters I have received from those people would have a better effect and carry a conviction to the minds of men stronger than anything I can say on the subject. I therefore forward you with this fifteen letters I have received from those persons, to do with as you think proper. Those letters were received by the way of New York, Philadelphia, Baltimore, London, etc., and have the post marks of those different cities on them, proving their authenticity. Should you determine to publish them, you might, if you thought proper, sir, invite all persons desirous of seeing the originals to call on you to see and read them.

In concluding this letter you will permit me to observe that the principal object I had in view, though I had several others, in assisting those people to get to their fatherland, was that they might there become the humble instruments of tending to the honor and glory of our divine Lord and Master.

And I confess their letters on that head fill my heart with joy and delight, informing me that they strive day and night in making known his glorious name and gospel among the heathen of that dark and benighted land. Some of them itinerate as missionaries of the gospel through and among the native villages, with marked success and blessings on their labors of love, and others keep schools among them for the instruction of their children.

With respect, I am, sir,
Your friend and obedient servant,
JOHN McDONOGH.

TO REV. ROBERT S. FINLEY.

New Orleans, June 15, 1847.

Dear Sir :—

Since addressing you on the 9th instant by mail, forwarding you a number of letters from my friends in Africa, I have copied the enclosed, being an extract from a letter of mine addressed last year to a friend in Virginia, which I promised to forward you when last here.

On looking over your letters to me, when here, on the 9th of April last, I perceive that your desire in obtaining a statement from me of the present situation and prospects of the people I assisted in going to Africa is to publish it with my first letter on African colonization in your paper, the Liberian Advocate. This I have no doubt would have an excellent effect.

At the same time it has struck me that were a large edition published in pamphlet form, commencing with my first letter as published in 1842, after that my account of the present state and prospects of those people, followed by their letters to me, (the plan of the Rev. Doctor Chalmers,) and closing the series with an extract which I now enclose you, (if you approve of its being published, and think it will have a good effect, or do good, all which I leave to your own judgment and discretion to determine on,) it would be a stronger mode to bring the subject home to the minds of men than by publishing it in detached pieces, as they would have the whole before them at one and the same time.

By distributing them in the different book stores, especially in the southern stores, throughout the United States, they would, I think, readily sell. You will excuse me, sir, in suggesting these things, and impute it to the true cause, the interest I feel in the separation, and consequently preservation, o the two races of men.

With great respect, I pray you to believe me to be, sir,
Your friend and obedient servant,
JOHN McDONOGH.

The Rev. Robert S. Finley, D. D.,
Saint Louis, Mo.

P. S. Did you obtain from the Rev. Doctor Scott, when here, as I recommended to you, the volume of Doctor Chalmers' works, containing a copy of his recommendation to the Parliament of Great Britain of the plan which I carried out with such complete success? It appears to me, sir, that on publishing the edition of my letters which you contemplate doing, were you to add the testimony, in his own words, of one standing so prominently before the world as that great man does, the effect would be conclusive and could not fail to bring conviction to the mind of all who read it.

As to my letters, which I send you, to Washington Mc-

Donogh, you could say, if you think any good would arise from publishing it, you found it enclosed in his letters to me, and that you have my consent to publish it, all which is the truth.

FROM JOHN W. S. NAPIER.

Dayton, Marengo Co., Ala.,
October 17, 1848.

John McDonogh, Esq.:

Dear Sir,—Please permit me to introduce myself to you as an inquirer after the success of the Liberians in Africa. I have been informed that you liberated some seventy or eighty slaves some years since, and sent them to Liberia, and that you would gladly give any information in your possession as to their success and prospects to any person who might wish to follow your example.

Knowing an individual or two who wish to be identified with the benevolent in that way, I wish you to give your views as to the result of such an enterprise. I find some fears as to their doing well even amongst those who are liberated, and any intelligence from you or those having experience would go to strengthen their hands. I received two pamphlets from the Colonization Society, the report of their last annual meeting, which convinces me of its benevolence and christian design and tendency. Your compliance will much oblige your friend,

JOHN. W. S. NAPIER.

TO MR. JOHN W. S. NAPIER.

New Orleans, October 30, 1848.

Dear Sir :—

Though covered with the affairs of life, and now old, I take a few minutes from sleep to acknowledge the receipt of your letter of the 17th instant and give to it a short reply, the brevity of which you will excuse.

The object of your letter is to ascertain the state of the late colony at Liberia on the western coast of Africa, now the free and independent United States of Liberia, or the Liberia nation, and how the colonists who emigrated from the United States, and especially those persons whom I, under the Most High, sent there, are pleased and satisfied with the country of their fathers.

Their prospects, as a great and happy nation, I am happy to say, sir,—as the pamphlet called the African Repository, which you inform me you have read, informs you,—are most flattering, being a republic with all its institutions modeled after our own constitution of government. The people composing it are, perhaps, sir, as my letters from great numbers of those I assisted to go there, show, one of the happiest communities on earth, wanting for nothing to add to their enjoyments of life and prospects of eternity.

They write me in short that they are happy, in want of nothing, having everything that they stand in need of in the greatest abundance, that the country is one of the finest on earth, the soil is extraordinarily rich, and climate fine for the black man, that they are owners of fine plantations, growing coffee, cotton, &c., &c.

Being requested last year (1847) by the Rev. Mr. Finley, who edits a newspaper in St. Louis, Missouri, called the Liberian Advocate, to give him some of their letters received by me, for publication, I gave him in consequence some twenty letters, which he published in that paper. Those letters were postmarked by the way of London, Boston, New York, Philadelphia, Baltimore, &c. The editor requested all persons interested in it to apply for the paper. I received a number of those papers, but have given them all away, or I would otherwise send them to you, sir.

But if you will address that worthy gentleman, and request the papers having those letters, he no doubt will forward them to you. It is a monthly paper, published at the low price of fifty cents per annum, which your friends might subscribe for, and which would give you every information of Liberia and its happy prospects.

I hope, and should be made happy in knowing, that the benevolent of your state had determined to assist the black man to reach the benighted land of their fathers, carrying with them the arts, civilization, and christianity of the white man of the land of their bondage, as the most glorious return we can make them for the injustice we have inflicted on their race.

With respect, I am, sir,
Your most obedient servant,
JOHN McDONOGH.

To Mr. John W. S. Napier,
Drayton, Marengo Co., Ala.

LETTER OF REV. R. R. GURLEY.

Washington, March 6th, 1850.

My dear and honored friend:—

Having some few days ago concluded my report in regard to the condition and prospects of Liberia, for the government, I avail myself of an early opportunity of stating to you, sir, as one of the truest and most generous friends of the cause of civilization and christianity in Africa, some of the impressions derived from my recent visit, and also some information concerning those who obtained their freedom through your kindness, and who on that far distant shore still cherish deep in their hearts towards you sentiments of gratitude, respect, and veneration.

I was for two months on the coast, and on shore almost daily, and had abundant opportunities to observe the character and operations of the government, and the dispositions and condition of the people. I have returned with a deeper conviction than I had before, that the scheme of African colonization is one of vast beneficence, meriting the earnest and liberal support of the whole American people. The Republic of Liberia promises to extend its renovating influence, and I have no doubt will finally attract to itself a large portion of our colored population, while it will gather many millions of the native Africans beneath the shadow of its wings.

A better ordered community it would be difficult to find, and one of the same number accomplishing as much good probably does not exist. There is, perhaps, less industry than there should be, but great improvements have been made, and there is increasing cheerfulness and hope and enterprise among the people, and this new aspect of things is to be attributed to their independence. What is most needed is some additional means to enable the government to explore the country, open new avenues for trade, make agricultural experiments, and improve the harbors and the system of education.

I saw a number of your people and visited their settlements on the beautiful banks of the St. Paul. Mr. G. R. Ellis is one of the most intelligent and respectable citizens of Monrovia, lives in a very substantial, well-furnished house, while he has a flourishing plantation some seventeen miles up the river. I visited him frequently. He has for his wife one of the best-educated women in the Republic, and is himself a man of great activity and enterprise. I am indebted to him for the following list of those who emigrated from your plantation.

George Ellis has a wife and two children. Jas. M. George (Taylor) is now living among the natives at Grand Cullo or Colo, engaged in the palm oil trade. I was at his house, and think that in regard to this world he is doing well.

Simon Jackson, Beverly Kelly, George Jackson, Augustus Lambeth, Joshua Johnson, Andrew Jackson, Washington D. McDonogh (now a missionary at Settra Kerro, married, much esteemed and doing well), John Martin, Charles Kelly, Charles Mason, Rhina Kelly (has seven children), Mary Jackson (has two children), Polly Jackson, Nancy Jackson (has two children), Polly Butler, Julia Lambert (three children), Molly Johnson (has three children), Henrietta Fuller (two children), Nancy Sturtevant (one child), Juda Smith, Rebecca Briggs, Matilda Briggs, Susan Mulcrease, Bridget Hyrer (one child), and Tama Morel. I presume this list is accurate, and I heard of no ill health among the entire number.

I am pleased to see that some movements are made in New Orleans to encourage and aid emigration to Africa, and I trust your own liberal example and your noble efforts will be imitated in all portions of the Union. I shall be happy to hear from you, sir, whenever your duties will allow you to write, and I pray you to accept the assurance that with the greatest respect I have the honor to be most faithfully your friend and servant, R. R. GURLEY.

TO REV. R. R. GURLEY.

New Orleans, June 10, 1850.
Dear Sir :—

A thousand thanks for your goodness in giving me the pleasing information you have communicated in your letter of the 6th of March last, in relation to Liberia and her prospects, and the people whom in the providence of God I had some little instrumentality in assisting to reach their fatherland.

If I have not acknowledged the receipt of your highly esteemed favor at a more early day, for it reached me in the due course of mail, it was because I was incapacitated by sickness from addressing you. I have had lately an attack of rheumatism, from which indeed I am suffering at this moment. For the last twelve months, however, I have not enjoyed my accustomed feelings of health, having been ill at ease without being sick. I imputed it to the closing of the seventieth year of my age, generally a critical period of man's life. Whether that was the cause or not, I cannot say. At any rate, with you, sir, I am assured in advance it will be accepted as a sufficient apology in not having sooner addressed you.

I heard of your departure for Africa and your return to your native land with feelings of the greatest satisfaction and joy, knowing that the grand object of your existence on earth, like your prototype St. Paul, is the honor of God and consequently the benefit and salvation of your fellow-men, and that, wherever you are moved, his honor and glory would be promoted by you.

Your opinion of Liberia and her prospects fills my heart with joy, and I agree with you, sir, "that the scheme of African colonization is one of vast beneficence, meriting the earnest and liberal support of the whole American people," and that Liberia will, as you observe, attract to her bosom a large portion of the colored people of our country. She must also receive in time, and that time is not far distant, the slave population of the south, manumitted and sent to their fatherland by their owners.

God in his mercy is preparing the means and the way. A few years more, and white labor in our country, from the natural as well as the foreign increase of our population, will be as cheap as it is now in France and Italy. Whenever that is the case — and it has been going down lower and lower for many years past — the slave holder will not retain his slaves, will not agree to keep and support them, but will drive them away, as white labor will then cost less than it would require to feed, clothe, and lodge his slaves, besides being in other ways more profitable.

The account you gave me, sir, of the moral and religious character of those people whom I assisted to get to Liberia, and of their happiness and prosperity there, affords me great joy. My first great object in assisting them to reach that country was the honor of our Lord and Master. To that end I strove to instruct them and prepare them, through a long series of years, day and night, and had them instructed in the knowledge of him and his righteous law. To know then, sir, that they are laboring in his divine cause with a holy and pious zeal, fills my heart with delight and thankfulness to him, the glorious author.

Can you inform me, sir, how and why it is that the missionary societies of our country look with apathy or coldness, if I may dare say, on the vast field of labor, heathen Africa, which is white for the reaping, and send no helping hands, no laborers to the harvest? Why, sir, are they not engaged in educating and preparing hundreds and thousands (if possible) of pious colored men for the African field, seeing that the climate is fatal to the white man?

Were seminaries established for that purpose, where black and colored would be educated for the ministry and supported free of expense, and advertisement made, I doubt not hundreds would respond to the call in a cause the most glorious of earth. Will the government of the United States do nothing in the way of an appropriation of money, say a half million of dollars annually, during the next ten or twelve years, to assist in the expense of transporting the free black and colored population of the United States to their fatherland?

The time I should think is a favorable one for pressing the subject on the attention of Congress. More especially as the great, virtuous, and good man, General Taylor, (who, without any information or knowledge of his views on the subject, I am convinced is favorably disposed towards it; for his heart is the seat of every noble, every benevolent affection,) is in the presidency. What subject is there, sir, after that of the Union, which interests more the American people than this?

A special message on the subject to Congress from the president, recommending at the same time the acknowledgment of the independence of the Liberian republic and the forming of a commercial treaty with her, would, I have no doubt, be acceded to by that body, and a law passed in conformity. I perceive, sir, in your interesting addresses delivered before the New York State Colonization Society lately, and before the American Colonization Society on the 15th of January last in Washington, that you advocate, as the form of government best suited for Liberia, that of a consolidated republic, in preference to a federal one or union of states.

You will excuse me, sir, if I mention this. It is not done to express an opinion, but to express merely my fears. The object of you and myself is the same, the happiness and prosperity of that people. You have reflected on the subject, and studied the people and their situation. I have not. But, as you observe, sir, she is destined to become a great nation, and to extend her sway over a great portion of that continent. In her present state of weakness, and for a length of time to come, no doubt, the most simple form for her would be consolidation.

But in time, when her limits will be greatly extended by

annexation, and her population increased by millions and tens of millions—for ambition fires the breast of the black man, as it does that of the white—would it not be found necessary, in order to satisfy her ambitious men, to have other high posts of honor, such as we possess in our different state governments, of governors, lieutenant governors, state senators, representatives, &c., &c.? Or would not their consolidated government be driven to the alternative of standing armies, which armies again in their turn would become most dangerous?

I have been taught to believe that the safety of our own glorious republic depended, under God, upon our federative system, the honors of our state governments acting as escape pipes for the high steam of our ambitious men to go off by and evaporate without danger to the body politic. You, sir, who have studied man as he is, and reflected much and deeply on the subject, do you believe that our happy republic would have descended from our revolution to the present day under a consolidated form, without shocks, attempts at revolution, or a large standing army?

I have not had the pleasure of hearing for a long time anything of the progress making in growth and other ways of your little son, John McDonogh Gurley. I hope he is everything that his parents' hearts can desire or wish him, and will become the support and consolation of their declining age. Be pleased, sir, to make my respects to your admirable lady, Mrs. Gurley, and with every wish for your health and happiness, and that of your family, I am, sir, with great respect,

Your friend and obedient servant,

JOHN McDONOGH.

Rev. R. R. Gurley, Washington, D. C.

MISCELLANEOUS

PAPERS OF JOHN McDONOGH.

FROM J. POGUE.

Baltimore, July 27, 1817.

Dear Uncle: —

I have it now in my power to inform you that last week the trustees appointed by the chancellor effected a sale of the whole of Grandfather's estate, and I think a very good one. The Market street property brought $17,100, and the remaining lots in the neighborhood of Grandfather's late dwelling, twenty-three in number, brought $11,500, a much better price than they did for at the mer sale. The terms of sale were one, two, twelve, and eighteen months.

There remains no likelihood of the estate being closed much short of two years. I cannot exactly learn the amount the estate is yet indebted, but it is not short of $10,000, so that a division of more than $1800 each may not be expected. Annexed you have the total cost of the Manor, by which you perceive how much I am in advance. It has amounted to rather more than I expected, but it is now well enclosed, comfortably improved, and will cost nothing further.

Aunt's family is now quite comfortably situated. She has four of her daughters at school, which is as many as can go at present.—Nothing new in this part of the world; times rather harder than usual. Our family and relations are all well.

I am, dear sir,
Yours sincerely,
J. POGUE.

TO MRS. JANE McDONOGH HAMETT.

New Orleans, March 2nd, 1834.

Dear Jane :—

I have your letters of the 26th July last and 13th of February, and note their contents. You speak to me of your son John, and say you have three sons at home whom you are anxious to place at trades. Then why do you not do it? Take my advice and bind them out immediately, let not a day go over your head till it is done. Immaterial to what trades, all are honorable. The carpenter, bricklayer, or blacksmith, if an honest, industrious, and virtuous man, useful in his day and generation and walking in the fear of the Lord, may consider himself the equal of the President of the United States.

Had I fifty sons, I would bring them up to hard labor and industry, giving them trades and nothing more. Even though I had it to give them, they should not have a cent from me. Bring up your children therefore, in the fear of the Lord, to industry and hard labor, and give them a trade. If they are virtuous they will find their way through the world. The Most High never abandons the virtuous man. We are here to labor, and from my experience I have found that happiness is only, at any rate chiefly, to be found in this world in the cabins of the industrious and virtuous poor.

With affection, your brother,
JOHN McDONOGH.

TO THE WASHINGTON LITERARY SOCIETY.

New Orleans, January, 1840.

Messrs. John M. Lowrie and I. Snodgrass,
Corresponding Committee Washington Literary Society:

Gentlemen,—Your esteemed favor of the 26th November last, by mail, reached me some time since, and I seized the first moment which my labors have allowed me since its receipt to acknowledge it and at the same time the high honor your society has done me in placing my name amongst its honorary members.

For this much of the good opinion of your society I return through you, gentlemen, my humble thanks, and beg leave to assure you, though I can do little for the advancement of your noble institution, that you do me but justice when you observe that I will ever wish to promote the interests of science, literature, and friendship.

JOHN MCDONOGH.

Lafayette College,
Easton, Penn.

FROM AUGUSTUS R. McDONOGH.

St. Louis, September 26, 1843.

Mr. McDonogh:

Sir,—My motive for addressing you will, I trust, excuse that freedom in one acquainted only with your name. Its identity with that of my father, the late Commodore McDonogh, attracted my attention some years ago, when I first became aware of your residence at New Orleans.

Upon being informed recently, since commencing the practice of my profession in St. Louis, that your native state is Maryland, I resolved to take the liberty of enquiring whether there exists any relationship between your family and that of my father, originally from Delaware, and of requesting, should that prove to be the case, the transmission of any information in your possession as to his early life.

It is scarcely necessary to add that the respect attending your name, wherever your late philanthropic conduct is known, would add greatly to the pleasure with which I should recognize any connection between it and my own. I am, &c.,

Very respectfully yours,

AUGUSTUS R. McDONOGH.

TO AUGUSTUS R. McDONOGH, ESQ.

New Orleans, May 20, 1844.

Sir,— I have the pleasure of acknowledging the receipt of your favor of the 26th September last, and owe you an apology for not having answered it long since. The cause has been my repeated absences from the city in different parts of the state, which put it out of my power to reply to it, and secondly, your letter having become displaced from the file of those I had to reply to, it was only this morning it caught my eye, which you will please excuse.

You enquire, sir, whether there exists any relationship between my family and that of your father, the late Commodore McDonogh. As I had answered this question some months since in reply to a letter addressed me from the city of Washington, D. C., by Mr. Thomas McDonogh, I will transcribe it here.

And with great respect I have the honor to be,

Your most obedient and humble servant,

JOHN McDONOGH.

TO MR. THOMAS McDONOGH.

New Orleans, July 31, 1843.

Sir,—I have received your letter of the 17th instant, wherein you enquire whether I am in any way related to the late Commodore McDonogh, of the United States Navy, and in reply have to observe, acknowledging at the same time as I do the compliment which the enquiry implies, that I know of no relationship between myself and that truly great and noble man, other than that which allies man to his fellow men of the whole human family.

And am respectfully, sir,
Your most obedient servant,
JOHN McDONOGH.

FROM THOMAS McDONOGH DUMFORD.

Lafayette College, January 24, 1846.

My dear Godfather:—

Some time since I took occasion to drop a few lines to you in conjunction with Messrs. Wood and Howell, corresponding committee of the Washington Literary Society connected with our institution, asking you to subscribe towards our diploma. I suppose you would have replied ere this to their demand if your business allowed you, which I took occasion to inform them.

But I assured them that they would beyond doubt receive an answer from you as soon as you could obtain leisure. I myself, I informed them, expected to hear from you also—the reason why I did not address you sooner than this. As I partially informed you concerning the object of getting a diploma plate, from which diplomas to be given to graduate members on leaving the society and the institution are to be struck off, I will say a little now on the subject.

In 1830 the Washington Literary Society of Lafayette College was organized and the constitution adopted. It was by a majority of the members seen fit to have something by which members could, after they left the body, be recognized, in whatever part of the world they may be cast. The latter plan of getting up a diploma was adopted, but never carried into effect, on account of the inability of the members to subscribe any large amount. Thus the matter rested for more than twelve years.

During the last summer I proposed to members of my class to urge the matter until they would accomplish the end which the constitution had in view. But the only answer I received was, "We cannot." "Very well," said I, "I will carry it on," and I proposed the plan of writing to honorary members for their support in this. We have thus far received one hundred and some dollars towards it. I firmly concluded that "perseverance conquers all things."

It will be a source of great benefit to the society and the institution, I think. It will be in the former case, in bringing a revenue sufficient to increase the library, which is one of the essentials necessary to the growth of an institution; and secondly it will induce members of the institute to graduate and receive their degree of Bachelor of Arts. The plate will cost about $140.

In conversation with our estimable Dr. Junkin, he informed me that in your last letter to him you had requested him to inquire of me of what profession I should make choice. I suppose he has already informed you of my intention of studying medicine. The study of physiology has always been a favorite of mine, either because it is one of the most perfect and complex studies, or the interest I have seen my dear father take in it; but one thing sure, I have always loved it.

The advantages which one has in pursuing this study far surpass those of the law. The law, permit me to say, is too much hacked up by pettifoggers and men of little wit. It is not made an object to improve the intellect, but a mere money making scheme. I think this should be as foreign to an individual's mind as possible, for it is impossible to improve the intellect when such an object is made the chief pursuit. Gain is mere nothing, if one does not gain what is useful. For many, indeed, have this in mind when they launch themselves upon the world, and alas, how many are forced to beggar the public. It is wrong, and should not be indulged in too largely. We live not for ourselves, but for God and mankind.

You will perceive, to your satisfaction, the provisions which I made and my calculations according to the orders of my father. He informed me that you had been sent my letter. I think that I come not very far from being right in my information. Where I shall study and when, is of course left to your discretion. I presume not to say, but leave it to your own proper judgment. You are aware that it is my last year in college, when I suppose I shall pay you a visit after so long an absence, and to those parents whom I so heartily love, my mother and sister.

I perceive that Judge Garland is in Havana, according to a letter written by a gentleman of New York to a Boston paper. He says a gentleman saw him in Havana discussing in a theater the Oregon, Texas and other questions. It is an awful strain upon the legal profession, from one too who stood so high in the ranks of his fellow men. May heaven guide him in his ways, and seeing his folly may he repent.

We had on Tuesday last a snow that fell to the depth of fourteen inches, but the weather after that began to get warmer, which causes the snow to melt very fast. The winter with us has not been very cold or heavy. Hoping that you will find a moment or two of leisure to address a few lines to me, and that the Most High will lengthen out your old age that you may in conjunction with my beloved parents once more allow me to look upon you there, I subscribe myself,

Your faithful and devoted godson,
THOS. MCDONOGH DUMFORD.

TO HIS SISTER MARY.

New Orleans, May 13, 1845.

Dear Mary:—In a letter lately received from your daughter Mrs. Hayne, she informed me of your loss, in the death, or rather departure from this mortal to an immortal state, of a son and daughter. In this disposition of the Most High, I I sympathize with you in your sorrow, and though, for short-sighted mortals, the decrees of an all wise Providence often run counter to our fondest hopes and desires, (and we know not why this should be so,) still let us have the head and the heart to bow in humble resignation to the divine will; for we shall know, see and confess hereafter that it was all in wisdom, and infinite goodness directed it for our eternal welfare in his everlasting purposes of love and mercy.

You, Mary, are not one of those who "sorrowing have no hope," but believe that our glorious Redeemer died and rose again, and that all those who believe in him shall rise also and be forever with him. Your children, departing on their journey in that faith which their pious father and mother had from infancy instilled into their souls, have only preceded you a few short days to that region of everlasting happiness where you will soon join them, never more to be separated, and where you will again meet in bonds of everlasting love those beloved and sainted parents, who to me, and I doubt not to you also, were beyond all things else on earth most dear.

We have the recollection, sister, of those beloved parents whom we shall meet again, and from whom we shall be separated no more, through the atoning blood of our blessed Saviour. If their children have been so wonderfully blessed in this life by the Most High, it has been for the sake of those parents in answer to their prayers. They reared us with such tender care in the path of virtue, and taught us to give our whole soul in love, first to the Divinity, then secondly to themselves, and lastly to our fellow man.

This never crosses my mind but my heart and my eyes offer up a tribute to their memory. Holding up then, my sister, in full view before your eyes the glorious command and promise, "Be thou faithful unto death, and I will give you a crown of life," let us press on to the end and secure that crown immortal and the joys which fade not.

I am, dear Mary, though old and advancing to the grave, still as in youth warm in affection for you.

JOHN McDONOGH.

P. S. Remember me to Mr. Cole, to your family, and to my beloved Jane.

www.ingramcontent.com/pod-product-compliance
Lightning Source LLC
Chambersburg PA
CBHW020139170426
43199CB00010B/807